Get Connected

Study Skills, Reading, and Writing

Ann G. Dillon
Austin Community College

THOMSON

WADSWORTH

Australia • Brazil • Canada • Mexico • Singapore
Spain • United Kingdom • United States

Dedication

To my brothers, Chuck, Bob, and Dan Dillon,

and my sisters, Patti Birckbichler, Liz Catalane, and Mary Jo Hutchison,

and all of my nieces and nephews, especially those in college.

This is for you.

Get Connected: Study Skills, Reading, and Writing
Ann G. Dillon

Publisher: *Lyn Uhl*

Acquisitions Editor: *Annie Todd*

Development Editor: *Maggie Barbieri*

Editorial Assistant: *Daniel DeBonis*

Marketing Manager: *Stacy Best*

Marketing Associate: *Kathleen Remsberg*

Marketing Communications Manager: *Darlene Amidon-Brent*

Content Project Manager: *Karen Stocz*

Senior Art Director: *Cate Rickard Barr*

Print Buyer: *Betsy Donaghey*

Text/Cover Designer: *Yvo Riezebos Design*

Photo Manager: *Sheri Blaney*

Photo Researcher: *Jill Engebretson*

Production Service: *G&S Book Services*

Printer: *Courier Kendallville*

Cover Art: © Oscar Knott/FogStock/Alamy

Printed in the United States of America

12 3 4 5 6 7 11 10 09 08 07 06

Library of Congress Control Number: 2006931945

ISBN 1-4130-3051-3

ISBN 13 978-1-4130-3051-8

Thomson Higher Education
25 Thomson Place
Boston, MA 02210-1202
USA

For more information about our products, contact us at:
Thomson Learning Academic Resource Center
1-800-423-0563

For permission to use material from this text or product, submit a request online at
http://www.thomsonrights.com
Any additional questions about permissions can be submitted by e-mail to
thomsonrights@thomson.com

Credits appear on page 154, which constitutes a continuation of the copyright page.

Brief Contents

Contents

To the Instructor

This text was developed to assist students in meeting the academic challenges of studying, reading, and writing in college courses. Many beginning college students are well prepared for and eagerly embrace the social challenges of attending college; however, only a small percentage of beginning college students are truly prepared for the academic challenges that they will face. In addition to traditional first-year students who have just graduated from high school, demographic changes continue to provide new opportunities for nontraditional college students: first-generation students, returning adult students, multicultural students, and students with disabilities. This text links essential skills and provides a solid foundation for all beginning college students so that they can achieve their goals.

Study skills, student success seminars, and first-year experience courses have become standard requirements in most universities, community colleges, and technical institutes across the United States. A majority of these courses focus on orientation topics, study skills, personal responsibility, and independence. While learning about study strategies is beneficial, in many instances study skills alone are insufficient to ensure success because college students must be able to read and write efficiently and effectively to earn passing grades in college courses.

For many beginning or returning college students, the cursory or ancillary treatment of reading strategies and writing techniques in study skills texts is insufficient to help them get connected with the strategies necessary for college success. This text connects studying, reading, and writing strategies and incorporates these essential skills into a text suitable for use in freshman seminars, provisional admission courses, readmission classes, developmental courses, workforce college programs, technical institute orientations, and returning adult student seminars.

The inspiration for this text is a product of my experiences developing and teaching integrated study skills courses and the desire to help all students learn to get connected with strategies that will lead to success. It is my hope that your students will learn to make the same connections among study skills, reading, and writing, develop confidence in their academic abilities, and form the bonds within your institution that will lead to successful completion of their higher education goals.

Organization and Features of the Text

This text includes several features designed to provide a foundation for students and flexibility for instructors. The first six chapters cover essential study skills, including goal setting, time management and motivation, learning preferences, critical thinking, note taking, and exam strategies. These strategies are intended to help students get organized and focused on success immediately and to be prepared to pass their first set of exams. While academic skills are essential to college success, there are a number of other factors that affect students' academic performance. Chapters 7 through 9 of the text address these issues affecting student achievement academically, professionally, and personally. The topics include communication skills, physical and fiscal fitness, and relationship building.

The text includes pre- and postchapter self-assessments, entitled "Are You Connected?" and "Have You Connected?" In addition, each chapter contains the following features:

Get Connected with Technology provides suggestions for using computers and technology to supplement and enhance traditional instructional methodologies.

Get Connected with Reading offers tips and strategies to help students focus on and get the most out of textbook and supplementary reading assignments.

Get Connected with Writing helps students to organize ideas and logically develop their thoughts to answer exam questions and complete writing assignments.

Chapters 1 through 3 cover four crucial study skills topics: goals, time management, motivation, and individual learning preferences. Within the context of these topics, Get Connected with Reading focuses on understanding reading and study systems, identifying topics and main ideas, and identifying major and minor supporting details. In addition, Get Connected with Writing provides a concise review of punctuation, capitalization, grammar, sentence structure, proofreading, and paragraph and essay writing.

Chapters 4 through 6 address critical thinking, taking textbook and lecture notes, and exam-taking strategies. The Get Connected with Reading sections in Chapter 4 through 6 cover critical reading skills, including understanding the author's tone, purpose, and intended audience, recognizing patterns of organization, and answering objective exam questions. Get Connected with Writing provides processes for mastering evaluative essays, patterns of organization, and essay exams.

Chapters 7 through 9 address the other issues that affect student performance: communication, physical and fiscal fitness, and relationships. As discussed in Chapter 7, students who can make effective oral presentations, understand nonverbal cues, and listen well are equipped with the communication skills for success. In Chapter 8, students learn about maintaining physical and fiscal fitness to ensure long-term success, personally, professionally, and academically. Finally, understanding relationship-building strategies in Chapter 9 is a lifelong skill that not only enriches the college experience but also prepares students to participate in the global economy. Get Connected with Reading in Chapters 7 through 9 focuses on point of view, evaluating arguments, and drawing conclusions, while Get Connected with Writing addresses persuasive and expository essays and research paper assignments.

Every institution of higher education is unique, and every student attending college is a unique individual. Although there is no magic potion to remedy every possible issue that these students will face in reaching their goals of academic success, my hope is that Get Connected will help you provide the tools for college success to your students.

Best wishes for a successful semester,
Ann G. Dillon

To the Student

This text will provide you with a foundation and the opportunity to practice skills and strategies that can help you succeed in college and beyond. In addition to learning study skills, this text also gives you a foundation for the reading and writing skills that are necessary for academic success. College exams generally include both reading and writing components. Regardless of how hard you study, if you are not able to express your understanding of what you have studied in an effectively and correctly written paragraph or essay, your grade will not reflect what you really know about the subject matter. Similarly, even if you have read the material assigned, unless you have taken good notes and applied critical reading and thinking skills while you were reading, you may miss points on exam questions.

Working with college students is a constant source of delight and an ongoing learning experience for me, as well as for the students in my classes. One of my personal goals is trying to help all of my students succeed in achieving their academic goals. This book will provide you with the skills and strategies that have helped my students. Students who understand and use study skills find that they can be efficient and effective students, but often study strategies alone are not enough to earn good grades in college courses. Although it may not seem fair that grammar, punctuation, and sentence structure count on political science or psychology exams, professors do deduct points for such errors. The same is true of college course reading assignments where professors expect you to evaluate, critique, or analyze information beyond the literal words in the textbook without providing instruction on the techniques that will help you perform this task.

Organization and Features of the Text

This text contains nine chapters with four sections in each chapter: study strategies, technology connections, reading connections, and writing connections. In addition, each chapter begins with an "Are You Connected?" prechapter self-assessment exercise and ends with a "Have You Connected?" postchapter self-assessment evaluation so you can check your understanding of the material covered. Get Connected with Reading sections in each chapter provide you with the reading skill sets that will help you read your college assignments more effectively and efficiently. The Get Connected with Writing sections in each chapter offer writing tools that will help you express what you know in the correct form and format on short-answer and essay exams.

The reading, writing, and study strategies discussed in this text have been extremely helpful to my students in transition to college, effective learning, college credit, and developmental communications courses. My hope is that you will learn to use and apply the study skills, reading, and writing strategies in this course to your other college courses and realize how much more effective you will be as a student.

Best wishes for a successful semester,
Ann G. Dillon

Acknowledgments

I have been very fortunate to have worked on this text with Carolyn Merrill and Annie Todd, Executive Managers, College Success, Thomson Wadsworth, and with Maggie Barbieri, Development Editor. Their experience, expertise, and insights have been invaluable resources, and I am grateful for the opportunity to work with them and benefit from their support. I would also like to thank Stacy Best for her marketing expertise. I also appreciate the support of Eden Kram, Assistant Editor, and Daniel DeBonis, Editorial Assistant, Thomson Wadsworth.

1 Setting Goals for Success

Setting goals for personal and academic achievements can help you plan, focus, and organize your college experience and achieve results. Those results—meeting your goals this semester—will serve as positive reinforcement for repeating the process each semester until you graduate. Perhaps most important, the goal-setting process will give you a framework for future success in the workplace.

In this chapter, you will first learn about the goal-setting process and how to develop short-term goals. You will also learn about reading and study systems that can help you meet your short-term goals this semester. Finally, you will focus on identifying common errors in capitalization, punctuation, and word usage that detract from your writing assignments.

Are You Connected? Self-Assessment

Answer the following questions by circling Y for yes or N for no. Revisit this assessment after you have completed the chapter to see if any of your answers have changed.

Y   N   **1.** Have you decided what grades you want to earn in your courses this semester?

Y   N   **2.** Have you developed a plan to help you earn the grades you want in your courses?

Y   N   **3.** Does your college sponsor an "Introduction to Using Technology" seminar or website?

Y   N   **4.** Do you have trouble concentrating when you read textbooks?

Y   N   **5.** Do capitalization, punctuation, and usage errors detract from the message you are trying to communicate when you write?

Learning Objectives

After completing Chapter 1, you should be able to demonstrate the following skills:

1. Understand the purpose and process of setting long-term, intermediate, and short-term (semester) goals and be able to develop well-formulated short-term goals.

2. Understand your institution's technology resources and requirements.

3. Understand and apply reading and study system strategies to reading assignments.

4. Understand the mechanics of writing, including capitalization, punctuation, and usage.

Developing Goals

Setting goals increases your chance for success. In many respects, goals are like dreams but with a dose of reality and deadlines added. Although you may dream of being a superstar, a billionaire, or a professional athlete, very few have the requisite talent, connections, or luck necessary to succeed at that level. However, you do have the ability to work in—and succeed at—a career in entertainment, business, or sports. When you set goals, it is important that you include reality and time constraints in the equation. Dreams often remain fantasy, whereas goals can be transformed into reality through a written plan that outlines specific steps aimed at reaching your goals. A degree and a career may seem distant when you begin college, but with a semester-by-semester plan to reach your goals, you can make them a reality.

The key to changing your dreams into goals is writing your goals down on paper—making a contract with yourself that you will have an obligation to perform. *Contracts* are written documents that transform vague promises into obligations, commitments that have built-in rewards and consequences. Writing goals down makes your fantasies more concrete, realistic, and achievable. In addition, the writing process helps you develop a *goal plan,* a map that shows where you are now and where you want to be in the future.

Types of Goals

Goals provide you with the rationale to do better, work harder, and achieve more. Goal setting is a process that you will repeat and reevaluate throughout your lifetime. You will meet some goals—earning your degree, for example—and then you will set new goals. You will reformulate other goals as circumstances in your life change. Some goals require a lifetime of commitment and effort. Goals are generally categorized by time frame—that is, the period over which you expect to accomplish them. There are three different types of goals:

Long-Term Goals

Long-term goals are sometimes called *mission statements* or *life objectives.* As these names suggest, these are goals you set to achieve during your lifetime. As circumstances change and time passes, you may revise, rewrite, or reevaluate your long-term goals.

Intermediate Goals

Intermediate goals are goals you want to accomplish in a three- to five-year period. Completing your certificate or degree program is an example of an intermediate goal. As the years pass and you receive your certificate or degree, save for and purchase a new vehicle, or qualify for and compete in a marathon, you will reformulate your intermediate goals to reflect what you want to achieve over the next three to five years.

Short-Term Goals

Short-term goals span a three- to six-month period. Your success in meeting your short-term goals affects your ability to reach your intermediate goals, which in turn has an impact on your ability to achieve your long-term goals. Short-term goals are also called *semester goals;* that is, they generally can be met in the time it takes to complete a college semester. Writing down your short-term goals can help you see what you want to accomplish this semester and then help you decide what you want to accomplish next semester.

To achieve your goals by the end of the semester, you have to be selective. Start with three items you want to focus on this semester, and work hard to achieve them. Taking on too much too fast will overwhelm you and set you up for failure. A better strategy is to work on three short-term goals this semester, three more next semester, and three more the following semester. For example, working on your grades, starting an exercise program, and joining a student organization this semester will keep you busy and give you plenty to think about and work on. Accomplishing three goals this semester is a much better strategy than undertaking ten goals and failing to meet them because you underestimated the amount of time and attention necessary to do so.

Writing Short-Term Goals

Step 1. Choose Your Short-Term Goals

The first step in writing your short-term goals is to choose them. As you think about your goals for this semester, consider the following guidelines to help you develop effective short-term goals. You can use the acronym SMARTER to help you remember the characteristics of short-term goals. Each letter in SMARTER represents one of the seven concepts you should keep in mind when you are writing short-term goals:

S: Specific

M: Meaningful

A: Accountable

R: Realistic

T: Timed

E: Empowering

R: Relevant

Be specific.   Identify the outcome or result you want to achieve clearly and definitely. Write your goals in positive terms that require more effort than just trying or hoping. For example, you might write, "I will earn at least a 3.0 GPA this semester" or "I will lose ten pounds this semester."

Choose meaningful goals.   Select goals that will make a difference in your life. Think about achievements that will make you proud of yourself at the end of the semester, and select them as your goals.

Be accountable for your goals.   Describe your goals and the steps to achieving them in terms that allow you to be accountable for meeting them on a weekly basis. Write goals such as "I will spend three hours a day Monday through Thursday and Sunday afternoon completing class assignments, studying, and reviewing." Then check each week to assess whether or not you studied on the days and for the time periods you set, make adjustments, and renew your commitment for the next week.

Be realistic.   Write goals that you can accomplish in the next three to six months. Setting goals that are too challenging or not challenging enough will have an impact on your self-confidence and your motivation. Goals should encourage you to do your best, but they should not be too difficult or too easy.

Set time frames.   Divide your short-term goal plan into daily, weekly, and monthly due dates, and on those dates assess your progress, revise your schedule as necessary, and recommit to achieving your goals. The key is not to let unanticipated events derail your commitment to succeed. Setting due dates can help you see what you need to do to get back on track when life intervenes.

Make your goals empowering.   Choose goals that will make you feel good about yourself and help you gain control of your future. For example, if you performed poorly in high school, setting and achieving a goal of an A or a B in a course can help you prove your abilities to yourself, boost your self-esteem, and motivate you to work hard in your other courses.

Choose relevant goals.   Select goals because they are important to you, not because they are valued by others. What do you want? If you write goals that are important to you, you will have a stake in achieving them.

Step 2. Write Your Action Plan

To use the power of goal setting, you must develop an action plan that describes not only your goals but also what you must do to achieve them. Writing your goals down makes them concrete and helps you to both visualize your dreams and commit to turning them into reality.

Your action plan should include the measures you will use to evaluate your success, any help you think you'll need, and the behaviors necessary for you to reach your goals by the end of the semester. If you anticipate problems that may prevent you from achieving your semester goals, identify each obstacle and specify at least one way to address or resolve it, or to minimize its effect.

You'll use the SMARTER characteristics to develop your short-term goals, but two of them have a bearing on your action plan as well. The first is being accountable for your goals by inserting *benchmarks,* some means of measuring your progress throughout the semester. Related to accountability are time frames. Again, you want to divide your action plan into daily, weekly, and monthly due dates, and on those dates assess your progress, revise your schedule as necessary, and recommit to achieving your goals. Remember that you want to identify problems while you can still solve them.

Step 3. Add Rewards and Consequences

You may find it helpful to build incentives into your goal plan. Think about rewarding yourself on a weekly basis for sticking to your plan. This may help you during the week when you are tempted to skip class, cut back on your studies, or not exercise. An ice cream cone, an hour playing video games, or a new CD can be a great incentive to keep you going when you feel like giving up. Similarly, imposing consequences, such as doing dreaded chores, can help motivate you to stay on track.

Get Connected with Short-Term Goals

In the practice exercises below, you will write short-term academic and personal goals you would like to set for this semester and then develop an action plan for achieving each goal. When you write your goals, remember to incorporate the SMARTER characteristics.

Practice 1: Short-Term Academic Goal 1

1. In the space below, write an academic goal you would like to achieve this semester.

_____

2. How and when will you know if you have accomplished this goal?

_____

_____

3. Will you need someone to help or support you in reaching this goal? If so, identify the person and the type of help or support you think you will need.

_____

4. What is your action plan? In the spaces below, list the actions you must take to reach this goal by the end of the semester.

_____

_____

_____

_____

5. Do you expect to encounter any obstacles in reaching this goal? If so, list each obstacle and at least one way to overcome it.

Obstacle   **Potential solution**

_____   _____

_____   _____

_____   _____

6. Are you going to give yourself a reward for sticking to your plan each week? If so, what reward do you have in mind?

_____

7. What consequence will you impose on yourself if you fail to follow through on your plan each week?

_____

Practice 2: Short-Term Academic Goal 2

1. In the space below, write another academic goal you would like to achieve this semester.

_____

2. How and when will you know if you have accomplished this goal?

_____

_____

3. Will you need someone to help or support you in reaching this goal? If so, identify the person and the type of help or support you think you will need.

_____

4. What is your action plan? In the spaces below, list the actions you must take to reach this goal by the end of the semester.

_____

_____

_____

_____

5. Do you expect to encounter any obstacles in reaching this goal? If so, list each obstacle and at least one way to overcome it.

Obstacle   **Potential solution**

_____   _____

_____   _____

_____   _____

6. Are you going to give yourself a reward for sticking to your plan each week? If so, what reward do you have in mind?

_____

7. What consequence will you impose on yourself if you fail to follow through on your plan each week?

_____

Practice 3: Short-Term Personal Goal

1. In the space below, write a personal goal you would like to achieve this semester.

_____

2. How and when will you know if you have accomplished this goal?

_____

_____

_____

3. Will you need someone to help or support you in reaching this goal? If so, identify the person and the type of help or support you think you will need.

_____

4. What is your action plan? In the spaces below, list the actions you must take to reach this goal by the end of the semester.

_____

_____

_____

_____

_____

5. Do you expect to encounter any obstacles in reaching this goal? If so, list each obstacle and at least one way to overcome it.

Obstacle   **Potential solution**

_____   _____

_____   _____

_____   _____

6. Are you going to give yourself a reward for sticking to your plan each week? If so, what reward do you have in mind?

_____

7. What consequence will you impose on yourself if you fail to follow through on your plan each week?

_____

Get Connected with Technology: Campus Networks and Websites

Make learning about the computer resources on your campus a priority during the first week of the semester. Take an online tutorial or attend a technology orientation on campus to find out about the following:

- word processing programs and the formats
- college and faculty websites
- e-mail accounts
- online and distance learning software
- campus intranet

Practice your computer skills and learn more about goals and goal setting by searching your college's online student resources, handbook, or website. The following are examples of resources that can enhance your understanding of goals and goal setting while practicing your online research skills:

- The University of Iowa's Academic Advising Center's website (http://www.uiowa .edu/web/advisingcenter/aac_curr_students/improving/motivation.htm) offers advice on writing goals.
- The University of Minnesota Duluth student handbook (http://www.d.umn.edu/ kmc/student/loon/acad/strat/goals.html) has information about and examples of goals.

- Idaho State University's website (http://www.isu.edu/advising/tips_goals.shtml) provides a form to use in setting goals.

Get Connected with Reading: Reading and Study Systems

To be successful in college at both your course work and exams, you must be able to read effectively and efficiently. Keep in mind that your main objective is to study harder, not longer. Many students use a reading and study system to help them focus and learn, and their success often is reflected in good grades.

You can use a number of strategies to create a physical and psychological environment that will enable you to concentrate more effectively on your reading assignments:

- Find a place to read where distractions are minimized.
- Choose the time of day when you are most alert and energetic.
- Read assignments before attending lectures.
- Divide long reading assignments into sections and read one at a time.
- Use a reading and study system and take good textbook notes.

Reading and study systems are effective tools that can help you focus on your textbook reading assignments. The five-step SQ3R (Robinson 1970) and S-RUN-R (Bailey 1988) systems prove effective for many students. SQ3R stands for Survey, Question, Read, Recite, and Review, while S-RUN-R means Survey, Read, Underline, Note, and Review. Some students, however, prefer the simplified three-step PQR system. As the name suggests, PQR involves just three steps: preview, question, and review.

- The purpose of the *preview step* is to get an overview of the assignment by looking at the chapter title, chapter outline, introduction, headings, subheadings, illustrations, and the summary or concluding paragraph.

- The purpose of the *question step* is to force you to read actively by pausing between paragraphs or sections to think about what you have just read and to ask yourself what the next paragraph or section will be about.

- You will be ready for the *review step* after you complete a section or a ten-page portion of a longer selection. Stop and review by summarizing—in your own words—the key ideas in the section you have just read. Or you can review by reciting the headings and describing the major points in each section. You can also review by taking practice tests or answering chapter questions.

Practice using a reading and study system on your next assignment in this course and see how much more focused you can become.

Get Connected with Writing: The Mechanics of Writing

Writing well is one of the most effective skills you can use to demonstrate your understanding and mastery of textbook and research material. Fundamental to effective writing is the correct use of capitalization and punctuation and the appropriate use of words that are easily confused—*their, there,* and *they're,* for example, or *to, too,* and *two.* Reviewing the capitalization, punctuation, and usage rules below will help you refresh your memory and avoid losing points on your writing assignments and essay exams.

Basic Capitalization Rules

Use capitals for	Examples
First word of every sentence	With luck, I'll get a good grade.
First-person pronoun	She and I are going away next week.
Proper nouns	a school in Boston
Specific persons and titles	James Dixon, PhD
Brand names, *but* not product types	Oreo cookies
Geographic areas, *but* not directions	I am from the Southwest; *but* I live east of the campus.
Newspaper and magazine titles	the *New York Times, The New Yorker**
Historical events	the Civil War (U.S.)
Specific buildings and institutions	the Empire State Building, Smith College
Religions, nationalities, and races	Judaism, African American; *but* whites and blacks
Days and months, *but* not seasons	Monday, September 4; *but* summer and fall
Specific courses with course numbers	Government 201; *but* a history course
Languages	French, English composition
Relationships without pronouns	I called Dad; *but* I saw my mother
Most words in literary titles	*Catcher in the Rye, For Whom the Bell Tolls*†

* Usually, but not always, the article *the* is lowercased in newspaper and magazine titles. Best practice is to check the publication's website. Another good idea is to keep a list of publication titles you've checked.
† The first and last words of literary titles are always capitalized—even articles, prepositions, and conjunctions.

Punctuation

The purpose of punctuation is to clarify writing: to communicate thoughts, ideas, explanations, and lists of items in meaningful form. When you speak, you use pauses, tone, and inflection to help your listeners interpret meaning. In writing, commas, periods, colons, semicolons, question marks, and dashes substitute for pauses and inflection. Proper punctuation will help you communicate your ideas, comments, and analyses clearly and effectively.

Review the rules and examples below. Then reinforce your understanding of how and when to use commas by watching how authors use commas as you read your textbook assignments.

Basic Comma Rules

Use commas for	Examples
Three or more items	long-term, intermediate, and short-term goals
Two or more reversible adjectives*	Writing is a difficult, tedious process; *but* red cotton shirt
Introductory phrases	Therefore, you are correct; Yes, I have the book here.
Direct address	"Your answer is incorrect, Sarah."
Geographic names and addresses	Rome, Italy; 2135 Mulberry Street, Springfield, Illinois
Specific dates	May 14, 2008, falls on a Wednesday; *but* May 2008
Titles following names	Nicole P. Baxter, PhD, will speak at the seminar.
Setting off quotations†	"I was able," he answered, "to write short-term goals."†
Clarification	For Brian, Michael is an excellent role model.

*Do not use a comma when the adjectives modifying the noun must be in a specific order. For example, the adjectives in the phrase "white cotton shirt" cannot be reversed without altering the meaning.
†Notice that commas and periods are placed inside quotation marks.

Punctuation Patterns

If you struggle to remember when and where to use punctuation to separate the phrases, clauses, and sentences you write, use the patterns below as a tool to help you visualize sentence structure and make the right decision.

Punctuation Mark	Rule	Pattern
Period	Use after an independent clause (a clause that contains a complete thought).	Independent clause.
Comma	Use to separate independent clauses joined by coordinating conjunctions (*for, and, nor, but, or, yet, so*).	Independent clause, coordinating conjunction independent clause.
	Use to separate an introductory clause (a clause that is not a a complete thought) introduced by a subordinating conjunction (*while, since, because, although, after, when, if*).†	Subordinating conjunction dependent clause, independent clause.
	Use to separate nonessential phrases or clauses (phrases or clauses that provide information that is not essential to understanding the sentence).	Independent clause, nonessential phrase.
Semicolon	Use to separate two independent clauses when the ideas are closely related.	Independent clause; independent clause.
Colon	Use to separate an independent clause from a list that explains or defines the concept in the independent clause.	Independent clause: item 1, item 2, coordinating conjunction item 3.

Commonly Confused Words

There are a number of words that students tend to confuse when writing. *Homonyms*—words that sound alike but have different meanings and spellings—often prove the most difficult because the spell-checking feature of word processing software usually does not distinguish between them. Studying the following list of commonly confused words can help you avoid making mistakes.

capital: main, funds, or city

capitol: building

it's: contraction of *it is*

its: possessive form of *it*

passed: past tense of the verb *to pass,* meaning "to go by"

past: time reference

than: used in a comparison

---

† Do not use a comma if the independent clause comes first, before the subordinating conjunction.

then: after

their: possessive plural pronoun

there: adverb that can be used to begin a sentence or indicate a location

there's: contraction of *there is*

they're: contraction of *they are*

threw: past tense of the verb *to throw*

through: preposition

to: preposition

too: also, excessive

two: the number

weather: climatic conditions

whether: poses a question

who's: contraction of *who is*

whose: possessive pronoun or interrogative pronoun

you're: contraction of *you are*

your: possessive pronoun

Proofreading

One of the best ways for you to check your understanding of capitalization, punctuation, and usage is to proofread your written work. Often when you are writing, you are putting down your thoughts quickly and focusing on the content, not the mechanics. Rereading the text you have written can help you identify and correct mechanical errors in your writing. You want your instructors to grade your papers on the content and presentation of your ideas, not on the errors you have made. Even when you use a word-processing program to check your spelling and grammar, make a habit of proofreading all your written work for errors that the program may have missed.

Have You Connected? Self-Assessment

After completing Chapter 1, answer the following questions about what you have learned:

1. What grades do you want to earn in your courses this semester?

   Course   **Grade**

   _____   _____

   _____   _____

   _____   _____

   _____   _____

2. What is your plan for earning the grades you want in your courses this semester?

   _____

   _____

3. List your professors' e-mail addresses:

Professor	E-mail address
_____	_____
_____	_____
_____	_____
_____	_____

4. What changes will you make to how you read in order to earn the grades you want this semester?

_____

5. Look at the last writing assignment your professor returned to you. How many capitalization, punctuation, or usage mistakes did you make?

_____

Chapter 1 Summary

Setting Goals for Success

1. Goals can be classified as long-term or lifetime, intermediate (achievable in three to five years), and short-term or semester (achievable in three to six months).

2. To be effective, semester goals must be specific, meaningful, accountable, realistic, timed, empowering, and relevant.

3. Once you develop your goals, you must write an action plan to achieve them and establish rewards and consequences for your success or failure at making progress.

4. Basic computer proficiency is a prerequisite to success in college; so is an understanding of the Internet and of the campus e-mail and intranet systems.

Get Connected with Reading: Reading and Study Systems

1. You must read efficiently and effectively to succeed in college.

2. Reading requires concentration so that you understand and remember what you have read.

3. Reading and study systems like PQR can help you read and study efficiently.

Get Connected with Writing: The Mechanics of Writing

1. College writing assignments require you to use correct capitalization, punctuation, and usage.

2. Capitalization rules govern the treatment of proper nouns, including brand names, geographic areas, historical events, buildings, titles, and languages.

3. Commas are used to separate words in series and to clarify other relationships between words and phrases.

4. Recognizing punctuation patterns in sentences can help you use periods, commas, semi-colons, and colons correctly.

5. Always remember to proofread your writing even if you use your computer's spell check and grammar check features.

References

Bailey, Nancy. 1988. "Beyond SQ3R." *Journal of Reading* 32, no. 2 (November): 170–171.

Robinson, Frank. 1970. *Effective Study.* 4th ed. New York: Harper & Row.

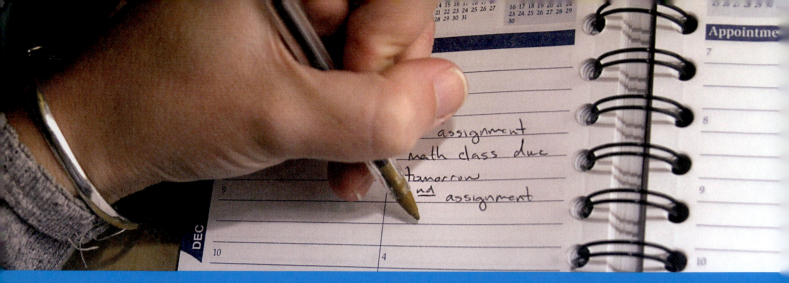

2 Managing Time and Staying Motivated

Successful college students manage their time well and are motivated to succeed. They keep their academic goals in mind and plan their weekly and daily schedules to allow sufficient time to prepare for classes, complete assignments when due, and study for exams. Contrary to the beliefs of many students, scheduling does not eliminate flexibility or stifle creativity. Instead, developing a schedule helps you deal with unanticipated events—last-minute emergencies and unexpected opportunities. Planning also provides you with quality time to enjoy social, recreational, and family activities without guilt or anxiety over academic obligations. Practicing time management puts you in charge of your time, instead of letting time control you.

   In this chapter, you will learn how to develop weekly and daily calendars and how to get help on campus from librarians, professors, counselors, and tutors to keep you motivated throughout the semester. You also will learn strategies to help you build your college vocabulary, identify topics and main ideas in reading assignments, and focus on writing complete sentences.

Are You Connected? Self-Assessment

Answer the following questions by circling Y for yes or N for no. Revisit this assessment after you have completed the chapter to see if any of your answers have changed.

Y   N   **1.** Do you know how to create weekly schedules and daily to-do lists to help you manage your time this semester?

Y   N   **2.** Have you visited your professor or a teaching assistant during office hours?

Y   N   **3.** Do you know how to use technology to manage your time and to build your vocabulary?

Y   N   **4.** Do you know what questions you should ask yourself to find the topic and main idea of a reading assignment?

Y   N   **5.** Can you distinguish complete sentences from sentence fragments, run-on sentences, and comma splices?

Learning Objectives

After completing Chapter 2, you should be able to demonstrate the following skills:

1. Understand and be able to create weekly and daily calendars and be able to use campus faculty, counseling, and tutoring resources to help you succeed.

2. Use technology and Internet resources to manage your time and improve your vocabulary skills.

3. Locate and formulate topics and main ideas in college reading selections.

4. Understand the essential elements of sentences and what constitutes a sentence fragment, a run-on sentence, and a comma splice.

Making Weekly and Daily Calendars

An old English proverb states, "What can be done at any time is never done at all." This adage is particularly meaningful for college students, who have so many things to do academically, socially, and personally. Unfortunately, at the beginning of the semester, many students often classify studying, writing papers, and preparing for exams as tasks that "can be done at any time"; then, at the end of the semester, they wonder why their grades are not better. In fact, one college professor jokingly proposed that a P grade—for "put off until too late"—be added to the typical A, B, C, and D grades (Rafoth 2002, 204).

As the semester starts, you may believe you are going to have time later on to complete assignments and study for exams. After all, the end of the semester is months away. So you procrastinate, deliberately putting off assignments and studying until it's too late to catch up, and you end up failing an exam, a paper, or even a course because you are not prepared. Scheduling and planning, using the calendars and strategies in this chapter, are valuable tools that will help you finish your papers and projects on time this semester and meet your academic goals.

Time Tracking

Time tracking is a helpful tool for you to use before thinking about developing your weekly schedule. The purpose of this time-management tool is to see what you do with your time on a weekly basis. You may be surprised at the amount of time you are wasting and the number of minutes and hours you can reclaim by being more efficient.

Figure 2.1 shows a weekly time-tracking worksheet. Use the following information to fill it in:

Activities: Review the weekly activities. Add any activities that are not listed that you do on a weekly basis in the spaces under "Other activities."

Estimated time: Estimate how much time you spend each week on each of the listed activities.

Ideal time: Write down how much time you believe you should be spending each week on each of the listed activities.

Actual time: Keep track of the time you actually spend on each of the listed activities over a one-week period.

Difference between estimated and actual time: Calculate the difference between your estimate of the time you spend on each activity and the actual time you spend on each activity.

Difference between ideal and actual time: Calculate the difference between the time you believe you should spend on each activity and the time you actually spend on each activity.

Remember that each week contains only seven days—a total of 168 hours. Your goal is to use them wisely.

Get Connected with Time Tracking

Make a copy of the worksheet in Figure 2.1, and fill it in over a week's time. What conclusions can you draw about how efficiently and effectively you are managing your time? After you complete your time-tracking worksheet, look carefully at how you spend your time, think about your academic goals for this semester (see Chapter 1), determine where your use of time is not productive, and plan to make adjustments accordingly when you are developing your weekly schedules.

Activities	Total Hours per Week per Activity				
	Estimated	Ideal	Actual	Estimated – Actual	Ideal – Actual
Eating					
Sleeping					
Dressing					
Exercising					
Commuting					
Attending class					
Studying					
Working					
Shopping					
Cleaning/doing					
Watching TV					
Playing computer games					
Sending and reading e-mail/surfing web					
Going out					
Being with friends					
Being with family					
Other activities:					
Weekly totals	168 hours	168 hours	168 hours		

FIGURE 2.1 Weekly Time-Tracking Worksheet

Weekly Schedules

A format to use for your weekly schedules is shown in Figure 2.2. Weekly schedules show the details of study hours, assignments, meetings, group study sessions, and appointments. A weekly schedule gives you a visual picture of what to anticipate for the week; it also tells you how much time is available for catching up on or rescheduling study hours, research, or work on assignments that are taking more time than anticipated.

With a weekly schedule, you can see which days are overscheduled and which days are underscheduled, and adjust your plans accordingly. You want to make sure that you have allotted enough time to study for all your courses, and that you've scheduled your studies for the time of day when you have the most energy and concentration. A weekly schedule also allows you to plan for eight hours of sleep a night, an hour of exercise daily, and time to relax.

Week of: _____

Time of day	M	Tu	W	Th	F	Sa	Su
6:00–7:00 a.m.							
7:00–8:00 a.m.							
8:00–9:00 a.m.							
9:00–10:00 a.m.							
10:00–11:00 a.m.							
11:00–12:00 p.m.							
12:00–1:00 p.m.							
1:00–2:00 p.m.							
2:00–3:00 p.m.							
3:00–4:00 p.m.							
4:00–5:00 p.m.							
5:00–6:00 p.m.							
6:00–7:00 p.m.							
7:00–8:00 p.m.							
8:00–9:00 p.m.							
9:00–10:00 p.m.							
10:00–11:00 p.m.							
11:00–12:00 a.m.							
12:00–1:00 a.m.							
1:00–2:00 a.m.							
2:00–3:00 a.m.							
3:00–4:00 a.m.							
4:00–5:00 a.m.							
5:00–6:00 a.m.							

FIGURE **2.2** **Weekly Schedule**

Get Connected with Weekly Schedules

Make a copy of the form in Figure 2.2, and fill out your schedule for the coming week. Be sure to consult your course syllabi for scheduled exams and for the due dates of projects and papers, and include time to begin studying or working on assignments on the days preceding the due dates. Use your campus calendar, too, to plan when you need to preregister or to start working on financial aid for next semester.

Daily To-Do Lists

Your daily to-do list shows what you intend to accomplish on a particular day. The main purpose of a daily to-do list is to enable you to set priorities, to work on completing the most important and time-critical items before tackling the items that are not as important or that do not need to be done immediately. For example, completing and proofreading a paper that is due the first thing tomorrow morning is a crucial item on today's to-do list: If you put it off until tomorrow, you won't finish your paper on time. Other items on today's to-do list might be to start work on a project due next week or to create this week's schedule. Both of these tasks are important, but not as crucial as finishing and proofreading the paper that is due tomorrow morning.

Get Connected with Daily To-Do Lists

Make a copy of the daily to-do list in Figure 2.3, and then fill it in with the things you need and want to get done today. Don't forget to check your weekly schedule for appointments and due dates. Now prioritize your activities. Is today going to be an especially busy day for you?

Today's date: _____	
Daily activities	**Priority**

FIGURE **2.3** **Daily To-Do List**

Getting and Staying Motivated

In addition to setting realistic goals and managing their time to meet academic goals, successful students are motivated to succeed. Motivation is what enables students to get on task and stay there throughout the semester. Motivated students look for and utilize all of the campus resources available to them for assistance, support, and encouragement throughout the semester. The faculty and staff on your campus are excellent resources to help you stay motivated.

Getting Help from Librarians

Although you may dismiss the library as low-tech or antiquated since you can research on-line, the campus librarians are among your most valuable resources to help you begin your research assignments, use databases, and locate the scholarly sources your professors expect you to use. If you have not yet taken a personal or virtual tour of your campus library, now would be an ideal time to see what is available and how the librarians can help you succeed this semester.

Getting Help from Professors

In high school, you saw your teachers every day; in college, you see your professors for just a couple of hours a week. If you have a quick question about material in a lecture or the textbook, or about an assignment, you may be able to ask it in the few minutes before or after class. If your question and the answer are going to take some time, you should make an appointment to see your professor during office hours.

You may also be able to reach your professor by e-mail or phone. When e-mailing or leaving a voice-mail message, remember to be specific about who you are, what class you are in, and what your question or issue is. A professor who receives a voice-mail message from "Michael in your history class and will you call me" probably will not. Information about how and when to contact your professor is in your course syllabus and on the department's web page.

Before you contact a professor, it is a good idea to make certain that your question is valid, that it is not something that has been explained in class, in the syllabus, or on the professor's web page. It is also a good idea to give your professor sufficient time to answer your question.

Professors can have hundreds of students and multiple obligations, which means it may take some time before they are able to meet with a specific student or respond to a specific e-mail. Don't wait until the afternoon before a paper is due to ask a question about it. Allow enough time to get an answer to your question and to take appropriate action based on that answer.

Your professors want you to do well in their courses and are interested in your learning experience. If you have a problem or a question, take the initiative and contact the professor or a teaching assistant.

Getting Help from Counselors

Campus counselors help students each semester with registration, course selection, and degree requirements. Scheduling is only part of their job, however. College counselors also can help you learn more about yourself through a variety of instruments that measure attitudes and aptitudes. If you're not sure what you would like to do for a living, or about the outlook for people in specific careers, a counselor can help you evaluate your interests and the opportunities available to you to pursue your interests.

Campus counseling offices also maintain part-time and summer job banks; coordinate on-campus interviews with employers; hold career and college fairs; conduct information sessions about scholarships, transfer, and graduate-school requirements; and provide lists and databases of community legal, social, and cultural resources for students. Counselors also arrange support groups, mentoring programs, service learning opportunities, and seminars for students on topics like stress, motivation, and time-management strategies.

Whatever your specific problem, issue, or question, a campus counselor can probably help you or refer you to the right place to get the help and support you need. Often students are unsure about important academic and personal decisions, and do not know where to turn. Counselors are great listeners who can help you find the best course of action to take.

Getting Help from Tutors

Most college campuses have learning centers equipped with computers, software, and textbooks for you to use. Learning centers also have tutors to help you individually or as part of a small group. Tutors often can quickly explain what you do not understand and work with you until you master the concept.

Working with tutors early in the semester is particularly beneficial if you are having a problem in a math, science, or foreign language course. If you wait too long before looking for help in these courses, you may become overwhelmed. Math, science, and foreign language courses are taught sequentially: You have to master the concepts and skills in one chapter of the textbook before you can understand the concepts and skills introduced in the next.

You can also visit the learning center tutors for help with assignments, papers, and projects in psychology, political science, English composition, or other courses that emphasize reading and writing. It is a good idea to work with a tutor on a routine basis, especially during the first semester or two of college, until you are comfortable with your course requirements and your professors' expectations. You can also turn to a tutor for guidance on a specific project. If you are having difficulty getting started or are uncertain about whether your writing meets expected criteria, a tutor can help you focus your efforts in the right direction.

Working with a tutor and meeting other students in the learning center who are also having difficulty can give you both academic and emotional support, helping you build confidence in your ability to learn and master college course content. Moreover, making

connections with resources on campus and other students who share your interests and difficulties can help you stay motivated.

Get Connected with Building a College Vocabulary

With so many things to do daily and weekly throughout the semester, it may be difficult to find the time for extras. One extra that you should make time for, though, is improving your vocabulary. Having a better vocabulary only takes a few minutes a day and will help you with both your reading and writing assignments.

Word Structure Clues

One way to add new words to your vocabulary is to make use of word structure clues—to look for Greek and Latin roots, prefixes, and suffixes that can help you decipher word meanings. For example, the Greek word *chronos* means "time." Words that begin with the prefix *chron-,* then, generally have something to do with time. A *chronometer* is a device that measures time; a *chronicle* is a straightforward account of historical events in the sequence in which they occurred.*

---

* Actually, there are two word structure clues in *chronometer.* The suffix *–meter* is from the Greek *metron,* which means "measure" (Merriam-Webster, 2003).

Word Context Clues

Context clues provide another way to add new words to your vocabulary. Textbook authors rely heavily on context clues in their writing to hint at word meanings. Among the most common context clues are the following:

Definition clues: Many authors of college textbooks formally define key terms as they introduce them. Key terms and definitions often are typeset in boldface or italic, or are printed in color:

> The term *chronology* is derived from Latin. *Chron-,* which refers to time, and *-logy,* which means "the study of," combine to mean "a statement of events in time order."

Synonym clues: Authors often use synonyms to clarify the meaning of new or unfamiliar words. Usually the new word or the synonym is set off by commas, parentheses, or dashes, or is introduced by *or* or a phrase such as *also known as* or *in other words:*

> *Bicentennials, or 200-year celebrations,* tend to be very elaborate.

Antonym clues: Authors also use antonyms to hint at the meaning of unfamiliar words:

> *Intermittent, as opposed to continuous,* studying is effective for many students.

Example clues: Sometimes authors use illustrations to hint at word meanings:

> *Biannual* and *biennial* are two terms that often confuse students. The prefix *bi* means "two" (a bicycle, for example, has two wheels). The word part *anni* means "year." *Biannual,* therefore, means "two times within one year." Some seminar courses are offered *biannually, once in the fall semester and once in the spring semester. Biennial,* however, means "once every two years." During a two-year period, a *biennial course is offered only once,* but a *biannual course is offered four times.*

Experience clues: Textbook authors can also reference a common experience to help readers understand what a word means:

> *Art, precious metals, and real estate tend to appreciate* in value over time, while *computers, cell phones, cars, and textbooks depreciate.*

Word Journals

Creating a word journal is another strategy to help you improve your vocabulary. A *word journal* is simply a list of words you've come across in your reading, research, or lab assignments that you did not know how to use, pronounce, or define.

When you encounter a new word in a text, mark or circle it, and then write or type the word in your word journal. Next, use your pocket, online, or electronic dictionary to look up the definition and pronunciation of the word, and write or type that information into your word journal. You can keep your word journal in a small notebook that you can carry with you. You also can create a word journal on your computer using a word-processing or spreadsheet program. The form of your word journal is much less important than how you use the document throughout the semester. To benefit from your word journal, you should review all the entries each time you add a new word. This review takes only a few minutes, but it is key to incorporating new words into your working vocabulary—an important semester goal.

Get Connected with Technology: Vocabulary and Time Management Tools

To help you master new vocabulary, check your college's learning lab or library website for a list of the commercial vocabulary-building software available to students. Among the commercial programs that many colleges purchase for student use are Lexia, Weaver, Plato, Destinations, and Skills Bank. Several of these programs have audio components, so that you can hear words pronounced correctly as you learn to decode and use them.

The Internet is another resource for expanding your vocabulary and for vocabulary references (dictionaries and thesauri). The following websites offer word-of-the-day games, dictionaries, and pronunciation guides that you may find helpful:

- Merriam Webster Online (http://www.m-w.com) features an online dictionary, a word of the day, and word games.

- Cambridge Dictionaries Online (http://www.dictionary.cambridge.org), a Cambridge University Press site, is a source for word games, idioms, crosswords, and worksheets.

- Vocabulary University (http://www.vocabulary.com) has word puzzles, crosswords, and root-word games at various levels of difficulty and in various subject areas.

- Bartleby.com (http://www.bartleby.com) defines a new word each day and offers a daily biography, quotation, and poem. The site also has links to a number of valuable reference books.

- Worldwide Words (http://www.worldwidewords.org) is a source for topical words and phrases, weird words, and articles on vocabulary.

Technology is also a wonderful tool for creating and tracking your weekly and daily calendars. Most computers and PDAs have time-management and scheduling functions, and many Internet service providers also offer personal calendar capabilities. If you use a computer or PDA on a daily basis, consider using an electronic calendar to help you manage your time. Here, too, the form—paper or electronic—is less important than what you do with your calendars. You should review and update your schedules every day to keep on top of due dates and other important deadlines.

Get Connected with Reading: Topics and Main Ideas

Topic, when used as a term in reading, describes the subject matter of a paragraph or larger text. A reading topic, like a title in writing, is not expressed as a complete sentence; instead, it is one or two words, a short phrase, or a clause that helps you identify the content of what you are reading.

The easiest way for you to locate or formulate the topic of a reading assignment is to ask this question: Who or what is this about? Remember your answer must be a word, a group of words, a phrase, or a clause—not a complete sentence. Textbook authors often use headings and subheadings to alert you to the topic that is discussed in the following paragraph or section. In a sense, the authors are doing the work of finding the topic for you.

When you are formulating topics for readings or headings for paragraphs and essays that you write, it is important for you to be as specific as possible and to make sure that your chosen topics or headings fit the reading or writing assignment. Although single-word topics and titles have a certain appeal, one-word topics can be too general. For example, the headings "Time" and "Calendars" are so broad that they fail to convey the actual subject matter of the paragraph or section. In contrast, a section title like "Time Management for College Students" or "Making a Semester Calendar" does a much better job of describing what the substance of the text really is.

The main idea is a statement that contains the topic and the author's most important point about the topic. To find the main idea of a paragraph or a reading assignment, first ask: (1) Who or what is this about? = topic; then ask (2) What is the most important point about the topic? This formula will help you remember how to identify main ideas: *Topic + Most important point about the topic = Main Idea.* In contrast to topics, main ideas are sentences, not words, phrases, or clauses. In addition, main ideas may be stated directly as a topic or thesis statement in an assignment, or main ideas may be implied in several sentences or sections of a reading. To form an implied main idea, combine words, phrases, clauses, or sentences from the assignment that contain the most important point the author makes.

Understanding topics and main ideas will help you understand and organize the information you are reading and learning and will also help you write the titles, topic sentences, and thesis statements for your own paragraphs and essays.

Get Connected with Writing: Sentence Structure

To write effectively about time management or any other subject, you must be able to write sentences that are grammatically correct.

Sentence Structure

Sentences are the basic units of writing. A *sentence* contains a subject and a verb, and expresses a complete thought. Sentences are also called *independent clauses.* "Sentences are the basic units of writing" is a sentence because it contains a subject and a verb, and it expresses a complete thought. "If sentences are the basic units of writing" is not a sentence; although it contains a subject and a verb, it does not express a complete thought. This is a *dependent clause:* It needs more words to finish the thought.

Sentence Fragments

"If you can work hard for only ten minutes" is a dependent clause: It contains a subject *(you)* and a verb *(work),* but the thought is not complete. As you read the words, you are waiting to learn what is going to happen if you work hard for only ten minutes. Adding the word *if* at the beginning of the clause changes the clause from an independent clause—which can stand alone—to a dependent clause, a thought that needs to be completed by an independent clause. In other words, "You can work hard for only ten minutes" is a sentence, but "If you can work hard for only ten minutes" is not.

The word *if* is a subordinating conjunction. Inserting *if* in the sentence "You can work hard for only ten minutes" makes the clause dependent; it is now a sentence fragment, not a sentence.

Since, because, as, before, until, unless, though, when, if, while, although, after, and *even though* are subordinating conjunctions. When these words appear at the beginning of a clause, they signal a dependent clause. When you use a subordinating conjunction in a sentence, make certain that you add an independent clause to complete the thought and the sentence:

> If you work hard for only ten minutes, you can finish several math problems or a section of a reading assignment.

Notice the comma separating the dependent clause from the independent clause. If you turn the sentence around, putting the independent clause first and the dependent clause second, you do not need to separate the clauses with a comma:

> You can finish several math problems or a section of a reading assignment if you study hard for only ten minutes.

Learning to identify the punctuation patterns described in Chapter 1 can help you avoid sentence fragments.

Run-On Sentences

A sentence fragment does not provide enough information to be a complete thought; a run-on sentence, on the other hand, provides too much information. Instead of a single complete thought, a run-on sentence contains two or more complete thoughts without separating them.

Consider the following run-on sentence:

> Work hard for only ten minutes finish several math problems or a section of a reading assignment.

"Work hard for only ten minutes" is one complete thought; "finish several math problems or a section of a reading assignment" is another complete thought.

One way to correct a run-on sentence is to use a comma and a coordinating conjunction—*for, and, nor, but, or, yet, so*—to separate the independent clauses. For example:

Work hard for only ten minutes, and finish several math problems or a section of a reading assignment.

Keep in mind that coordinating conjunctions are also used to connect multiple items in a list ("semester, weekly, *and* daily calendars") and to form compound subjects ("students *or* professors") and compound verbs ("has planned *or* scheduled").

Another way to correct a run-on sentence is to separate the independent clauses with a semicolon:

Work hard for only ten minutes; finish several math problems or a section of a reading assignment.

Again, learning punctuation patterns, like the patterns in Chapter 1, will help you avoid writing run-on sentences.

Comma Splices

In a comma splice, two independent clauses are separated by just a comma, with no coordinating conjunction. In other words, a comma splice is a run-on sentence with a comma:

Work hard for only ten minutes, finish several math problems or a section of a reading assignment.

Here, too, you have two options. You can add a coordinating conjunction (*for, and, nor, but, or, yet, so*) after the comma:

Work hard for only ten minutes, and finish several math problems or a section of a reading assignment.

Alternatively, you can replace the comma with a semicolon:

Work hard for only ten minutes; finish several math problems or a section of a reading assignment.

Here, too, understanding punctuation patterns in Chapter 1 can help you correct and avoid writing comma splices.

Have You Connected? Self-Assessment

After completing Chapter 2, answer the following questions about what you have learned:

1. Do you have the following tools on paper or in electronic form to help you manage your time this semester?

   Y N   Weekly schedule

   Y N   Daily to-do list

2. Where and when are your professors available to meet with you?

_____

3. How will you use technology to help you manage your time and build your vocabulary?

_____

4. What questions should you ask to help you find the topic and main idea of a college reading assignment?

_____

_____

5. Define and give an example of each of the following:

a. Sentence _____

_____

b. Sentence fragment _____

_____

c. Run-on sentence _____

_____

d. Comma splice _____

_____

Chapter 2 Summary

Managing Time and Staying Motivated

1. Creating written weekly and daily calendars will help you plan and manage your time wisely during the semester.

2. Weekly schedules allow you to plan ahead and avoid conflicts and last minute crises when you have multiple crucial tasks to complete. Daily to-do lists are essential to prioritizing your activities.

3. Campus resources including librarians, professors, counselors, and tutors are available to help you succeed, stay motivated, and reach your goals.

4. Websites that offer dictionaries, a word of the day, or word games can help you expand your vocabulary, which in turn will make you a more effective reader and writer.

Get Connected with Reading: Topics and Main Ideas

1. Topics are words or phrases that describe the specific subject matter of a reading selection.

2. To identify the topic of a paragraph or selection, ask "Who or what is this about?"

3. To identify the main idea of a paragraph or selection use this formula:
Topic + Most important point about the topic = Main idea.

Get Connected with Writing: Sentence Structure

1. A sentence, or independent clause, contains a subject and a verb, and it expresses a complete thought.

2. Sentence fragments are dependent clauses: They contain a subject and a verb, but do not express a complete thought. A subordinating conjunction at the start of a clause signals a dependent clause. To fix a sentence fragment, you must add an independent clause.

3. Run-on sentences combine two independent clauses. You can correct a run-on sentence by inserting a comma and a coordinating conjunction, or a semicolon, between the two clauses.

4. A comma splice is a series of two (or more) independent clauses separated by commas (with no coordinating conjunction). You can fix a comma splice by adding a coordinating conjunction, or by replacing the comma with a semicolon.

References

Merriam-Webster's Collegiate Dictionary. 2003. 11th ed. CD-ROM. Merriam-Webster.

Rafoth, Ben. 2002. "A Question of Procrastination or Ineptitude." *Journal of College Reading and Learning* 32, no. 2 (Spring): 204–210.

3 Individual Learning Preferences

To succeed in college, you must develop learning strategies that maximize your strengths and limit the impact of your weaknesses. The subject of this chapter is individual learning preferences. Understanding your sensory, cognitive, and social learning styles can lead you to specific study strategies that can maximize your academic performance, helping you complete assignments, study, and prepare for exams more effectively and efficiently.

In this chapter, you will learn about several types of learning preferences and assess your own personal preferences. In addition, you will learn how to identify details in college reading assignments, which will help you answer objective exam questions and focus your attention on writing well-constructed paragraphs and essays that incorporate details.

Are You Connected? Self-Assessment

Answer the following questions by circling Y for yes or N for no. Revisit this assessment after you have completed the chapter to see if any of your answers have changed.

Y   N   **1.** Do you know what your sensory learning preference is?

Y   N   **2.** Do you know what your cognitive and social learning preferences are?

Y   N   **3.** Have you visited different websites to familiarize yourself with learning preference inventories?

Y   N   **4.** Do you know what questions to ask yourself when you are looking for major and minor details in a reading assignment?

Y   N   **5.** Do you know how to organize and write paragraphs and essays?

Learning Objectives

After completing Chapter 3, you should be able to demonstrate the following skills:

1. Understand sensory, cognitive, and social learning preferences and their academic value.

2. Apply study strategies that reflect your learning preferences and enhance your learning.

3. Locate and identify major and minor details in college readings.

4. Understand the organization and essential elements of paragraphs and essays.

Understanding Individual Learning Preferences

People learn in different ways, which explains, at least in part, why you prefer certain learning activities over others. From experience you probably know what you do well at and what you don't. But do you know why you like lectures and not labs? Or why you enjoy reading alone but dislike group discussions? At work here are your individual learning preferences, your responses to your individual strengths and weaknesses. Learning preferences are just that, the ways you prefer to learn, the ways you are more comfortable learning. But just because you prefer to learn by hearing information, for example, does not mean that you cannot learn by reading a textbook; it simply means that you would rather listen than read.

Learning Preference Inventories

There are a number of formal and informal *inventories*—tests that have no right or wrong answers—that can help you identify your individual strengths and weaknesses. You can learn more about these inventories, and even take some of them, at your campus counseling center or on the Internet. The results of these inventories can help you assess your strengths and weaknesses as a student; many include suggestions and strategies to help you study more effectively and do better in your course work.

Learning preference inventories generally are divided into three types: sensory, cognitive, and social. Inventories of sensory learning preferences explain how you receive information; cognitive inventories explain the functions you use to process that information; and social learning inventories explain the conditions under which you learn best—studying alone or in a group, for example.

Measures of Sensory Learning Preferences

You acquire information through your senses. In school, you generally rely on three senses: sight, sound, and touch. Your learning, then, is visual, auditory, and tactile:

- *Visual learning* is what is going on when you read a textbook, look at slides or transparencies, or study a graph.
- *Auditory learning* is at work when you listen to a professor's lecture or to an audiotape.
- *Tactile learning,* or *kinesthetic learning,* is at work when you touch a substance in a lab or use a computer. Tactile learners learn best through hands-on or do-it-yourself activities.

Measures of Cognitive Learning Preferences

You acquire information through your senses; you process and incorporate it primarily through four types of cognitive learning:

- *Analytical learning* focuses on facts.
- *Innovative learning* relies more on personal feelings and reactions.
- *Dynamic learning* is often a process of self-discovery.
- *Commonsense learning* is based on a need to understand how things work.

Measures of Social Learning Preferences

The results of a third type of inventory—social learning scales—can be used to understand why you learn better in certain situations than in others. These scales tend to focus on motivation and attitude to explain students' responses to the learning environment. You might find the results of a social learning inventory particularly helpful if you are considering taking a distance-learning course. If your score on the inventory indicates that you learn best through interaction, discussion, and collaboration, distance learning may not give you the social contact you need to learn most effectively (Diaz and Cartnal 1999, 131–133). And professors often use the results of social learning scales to adapt the learning environment, the content, and their methods to students' learning styles.

Get Connected with Sensory Learning Preferences

What type of sensory learner are you? Use the checklists below to assess your sensory learning preferences. In each, place a check mark in front of the characteristics that describe you. Then add the total number of check marks you made in each of the three checklists. The list with the most check marks reflects your primary sensory learning preference; the list with the next highest number of check marks, your secondary sensory learning preference.

Visual Learner Checklist

_____ You remember what you see or read.

_____ You prefer information to be presented visually.

_____ You prefer your professors to use blackboards, slides, or transparencies.

_____ You care about how things look.

_____ You think color is important.

_____ You like making lists.

_____ You often ask that oral information be repeated.

_____ You like to read.

Total number of check marks: _____

Auditory Learner Checklist

_____ You remember what you hear.

_____ You talk to yourself as you write.

_____ You do not like to read very much.

_____ You remember music.

_____ You have difficulty following written instructions.

_____ You do not write legibly.

_____ You are a good speaker.

Total number of check marks: _____

Tactile Learner Checklist

_____ You like field experiences.

_____ You prefer courses with labs.

_____ You like to be physically active when studying.

_____ You remember by doing things.

_____ You are a good athlete or dancer.

_____ You handle or touch things to learn.

_____ You do not like to read very much.

Total number of check marks: _____

Sensory Learning Strategies

Whatever your sensory learning style, there are a number of strategies you can use to improve your learning and studying skills.

    Visual learners, for example, should focus on the following strategies:

- Make notes about the slides, transparencies, and other graphics used in class.
- Color-code new information using highlighters or colored pens and pencils.
- Pay attention to photographs, charts, graphs, and diagrams in the textbook when you study.
- Watch videotapes.
- Write summaries of what you have read.
- Make note cards to study.
- Visualize information when you read.
- Write down information you are trying to learn on Post-It notes, and put the notes everywhere—along the edges of your computer monitor, on a mirror, on the refrigerator, on your pillow.

Auditory learners should focus on the following strategies:

- Read important information from your textbook out loud.
- Record your professors' lectures and listen to the tapes for review.
- Use books on tape.
- Join a study group.
- Talk to yourself as you go through the steps, processes, and information that you are learning.
- Verbalize information to yourself as you write it down.
- Make up songs, rhymes, or verses to learn information.
- Create your own audiotapes when you study, and play them back for review.

Tactile learners should focus on the following strategies:

- Read with the textbook in your hands.
- Sit in the front of the class so that you stay involved.
- Use a computer to take and review notes.
- Stand up and walk around when you read.
- Read while you are using an exercise bike, a treadmill, or a stair-stepper.
- Attend all labs.
- Make note cards and sort them into stacks when you are studying.
- Chew gum when you study.

Understanding the type of learner you are—visual, auditory, or tactile—will help you focus on your strengths in class when you are watching, listening, and taking notes. For example, if you are a visual learner, you will know to sit in the front of the classroom so that you can see the professor and the board clearly. If you are an auditory learner, you can plan to bring a tape recorder with you to class, to tape lectures and discussion. If you are a tactile learner, you will know that it's especially important for you to make it to every lab.

Understanding sensory learning preferences may also give you insight into your classmates' behaviors. You may continue to feel annoyed by the student sitting next to you who keeps tapping her pencil or the student in front of you who is chewing gum loudly; but now, at least, you will understand that they are not trying to bother you. You may just be sitting near a couple of tactile learners.

Cognitive Learning Preferences

Cognitive learning refers to how you process the information you acquire through sight, sound, and touch. It describes how you think about and use information. Again, there are four different styles of cognitive processing:

Analytical Learning

Analytical learners like to think about concepts and ideas. They tend to collect and analyze information before making decisions. For courses, they enjoy math, physics, chemistry, and accounting; they like objective exams that ask true-false, multiple-choice, or problem-solving

questions. Most analytical learners would opt for a lecture course, with visual aids, over a lab. And most prefer studying alone.

Innovative Learning

If analytical learners are rational, innovative learners are emotional: They tend to base their decisions on their feelings and their personal values. Their favorite courses include social sciences and behavioral sciences; they much prefer subjective exams that require written answers in which they can discuss and explain their position. Innovative learners like being with other people, a trait that explains their enjoyment of both class discussions and study groups.

Dynamic Learning

Dynamic learning involves taking risks. Dynamic learners are flexible; in fact, they look for opportunities to vary their routines, and they adapt easily to change. They tend to learn through self-discovery and trial and error. They like looking for hidden possibilities; for them, discovering the correct answers is more important than understanding the process involved in determining those answers. They enjoy taking courses in business, marketing, and sales, and they learn best through role-play, simulation, and independent projects.

Commonsense Learning

Commonsense learners like to know how things work. They like to use facts to build concepts and then test those concepts. Not surprisingly, then, they learn best through their sense of touch—the kinds of hands-on learning characteristic of lab courses. Commonsense learners tend to take classes in computer science, engineering, and health science—courses that offer fieldwork, computer simulations, and demonstration lectures. Like analytical learners, these learners prefer objective exams.

Which of the four cognitive learning styles best describes you? Understanding your cognitive learning style will help you focus on study and learning strategies that suit your individual way of learning. It can also help you choose your courses in terms of both format (lecture, seminar, lab) and subject matter (math, social science, business, health science) to enhance your individual learning style.

In addition, familiarity with cognitive learning styles will help you understand how others think and act. For example, realizing that your cognitive learning preference is innovative and that your professor's is analytical may help you understand your frustration with a course. Although you may not be able to do anything about how your professor presents material, understanding your problems with the professor's methods may well help you come up with ideas about how to study more effectively.

Get Connected with Cognitive Learning Preferences

What is your cognitive learning preference? Use the checklists below to find out. In each list, place a check mark in front of the activities you enjoy. Then total the number of check marks you have made. When you've finished, use the totals to rank your cognitive learning preferences.

Analytical Learning Checklist

_____ Looking for facts

_____ Thinking about concepts and ideas

_____ Collecting and analyzing information before making decisions

_____ Taking exams that ask true/false, multiple-choice, or problem-solving questions

_____ Taking courses in math, physics, chemistry, and accounting

_____ Learning in lecture courses with visual aids

_____ Studying alone

Total number of check marks: _____

Innovative Learning Checklist

_____ Using personal feelings to make decisions

_____ Interacting with other people

_____ Relying on your personal values

_____ Taking subjective exams that require written answers in which you can discuss and explain your position

_____ Taking courses in social sciences and behavioral sciences

_____ Learning in courses that use a class discussion format

_____ Studying with study groups

Total number of check marks: _____

Dynamic Learning Checklist

_____ Looking for hidden possibilities when you process information

_____ Learning through self-discovery and trial and error

_____ Making changes in your routines

_____ Being flexible and taking risks

_____ Discovering the correct answers without knowing the exact process

_____ Taking courses in business, marketing, and sales

_____ Learning through role-playing, simulations, and independent projects

Total number of check marks: _____

Commonsense Learning Checklist

_____ Discovering how things work

_____ Using facts, building concepts, and testing your concepts

_____ Using sensory experiences to make your decisions

_____ Taking skills-oriented and hands-on learning or lab courses

_____ Taking exams that ask true-false, multiple-choice, or problem-solving questions

_____ Taking courses in computer science, engineering, and health sciences

_____ Taking courses that have a fieldwork component or make use of computer simulations and demonstrations

Total number of check marks: _____

Ranking Your Preferences

Now use the totals from each of the four checklists to rank your cognitive learning preferences. Number 1 should be the style with the most check marks and number 4 the style with the fewest check marks.

Cognitive Learning Preference Rank

_____ Analytical

_____ Innovative

_____ Dynamic

_____ Commonsense

Finally, review the descriptions and checklists for your two highest-ranked preferences, and think about the learning strategies and the courses (format and content) suggested there.

In the spaces below, write two strategies you might adopt to fit each of those preferences.

Strategies for cognitive learning preference 1: _____

_____

Strategies for cognitive learning preference 2: _____

_____

Social Learning Preferences

Your social learning preferences determine the conditions under which you study and learn most effectively. For example, some students thrive on competition, doing their best work when they can gauge their progress against that of another student. These students obviously learn better in a group situation . . . as long as at least one member of the group offers competition. These students also respond well to recognition and other rewards for work well done.

Other students enjoy the interaction in a class discussion or study group: They are motivated by collaboration, not competition. Social group learners master material by participating in group discussions. They like to ask questions of tutors and other students while studying. Group learners often study in learning centers and student lounges, where discussion is allowed. Distance learning is difficult for these learners because working online does not give them the interaction they need to study and learn most effectively.

Individual social learners prefer to study alone and often set up their schedules to study when no one else is around. They cannot concentrate where there is noise around them, which is why they often study in the quiet of the campus library. When they have a question on material, they tend to write it down and then follow up later with their professor, a teaching assistant, or a tutor. Individual learners usually thrive in distance learning because neither social interaction nor discussion is essential to their learning process.

Are you a group or an individual learner? Many students find study groups an excellent way to share and learn productively. Study groups are particularly helpful for first-year college students, who often struggle until they understand how to study effectively and how college exams are structured. However, if you have trouble concentrating amid noise or other distractions, or if you simply like to be alone, you probably won't get much out of a study group, and you may find group projects extremely frustrating. Your social learning preference can help you decide whether or not to join a voluntary study group or take an online course, and to understand how you can make adjustments when you work with others who learn and study differently from you.

Table 3.1 is a summary of sensory, cognitive, and social learning preferences. Circle the entry in each column that best describes you. Reviewing your choices will give you a more complete understanding of how you study and learn most effectively.

TABLE **3.1**   **Summary of Learning Preferences**

Sensory Learning	Cognitive Learning	Social Learning
Visual: looking at books or visual aids	Analytical: relying on facts and proof	Individual: studying and learning alone
Auditory: hearing lectures or tapes	Innovative: using personal feelings	Group: learning through discussion with others
Tactile: touching or moving materials	Dynamic: enjoying self-discovery and new possibilities	
	Commonsense: relying on hands-on and field experiences	

Get Connected with Technology: Online Inventories

You can learn more about your learning preferences on the Internet. There are a number of online inventories that you can take and submit to receive your results instantaneously.

VARK (http://www.vark-learn.com), for example, is an assessment of sensory learning styles, and it offers strategies for each learning preference. Many college websites also offer assessments of learning preference and suggestions for study strategies. The University Learning Center at the University of Arizona (http://www.ulc.arizona.edu/learning_style.php) and Brookhaven College (http://www.brookhavencollege.edu/learningstyle/modality_test.html) are examples.

Other good sites include the following:

- Learning Done Your Way (http://library.thinkquest.org/TQ0310722/TQ0310722.html) offers an interactive quiz based on Howard Gardner's theory of multiple intelligences. The quiz can help you identify your strongest and weakest domains.
- For information about the Keirsey Temperament Sorter, check http://www.keirsey.com.
- Brevard College's Policy Center on the First Year of College (http://www.brevard.edu/fyc/resources/Learningstylesinstruments.htm) has a list of twenty learning style assessments, including the Gregorc Style Delineator, the Kolb Learning Style Inventory, and the Myers-Briggs Type Indicator.
- The Personality Page (http://www.personalitypage.com/careers.html) describes common career choices for the various Myers-Briggs types.

Get Connected with Reading: Major and Minor Details

Reading for details is a skill you will rely on throughout your college experience. Obviously, recognizing facts, examples, definitions, and explanations adds to your understanding of a subject. In addition, knowing how to locate and identify details in what you are reading will help you when you have to structure your own writing in both assignments and essay exams.

And, of course, most of the questions on your objective exams—true/false, multiple-choice, matching, and fill-in-the-blanks—will test your recall and understanding of the details in your reading assignments.

The main idea is the broad, general statement that covers all of the specific ideas, thoughts, and examples in a paragraph or reading selection (see Chapter 2). Details are the specific ideas, thoughts, and examples that support and prove the validity of the main idea. Typically, details include the following types of information: names, definitions, dates, reasons, descriptions, steps, statistics, and sequences.

Authors often use introductory words to signal to their readers that they are about to cite a detail. Among those words are *first* or *(1), second* or *(2), third* or *(3), in addition, also, for example, next, then, last,* and *finally.* Details generally are classified as either major or minor. That classification is based on whether a detail supports the main idea or explains another detail.

Major Details

Major details directly support the main idea: There is a direct relationship between major details and the main idea. When you need to locate the major details in a reading assignment, ask yourself this question: "What else does the author want me to know about the main idea?" There is no formula to help you determine the number of major details in a paragraph or reading assignment. Whereas you know that every paragraph can have just one topic and just one main-idea sentence, in theory, at least, there is no limit to the number of major details in any one paragraph.

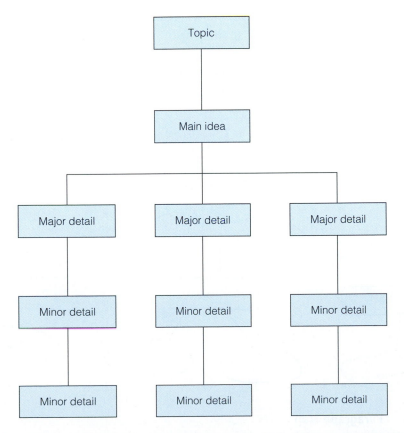

FIGURE **3.1**   **Relationship of Minor Details to Topic, Main Idea, and Major Details**

Minor Details

Minor details do not support or relate to the main idea directly. Instead, minor details provide you with explanations, examples, and illustrations that help you understand the major details in your reading assignments, which in turn help you focus on the main idea. The relationships among topic, main idea, major details, and minor details are illustrated in Figure 3.1.

Here, too, there is no pattern or formula that will tell you how many minor details are in a reading assignment. However, you can distinguish between major and minor details by asking yourself this question: "Does this detail support or explain a major detail instead of the main idea?" If your answer is yes, then the detail is a minor detail. If your answer is no, then ask, "Does this detail directly relate to or explain the main idea?" If so, then the detail is a major detail.

Get Connected with Writing: Paragraphs and Essays

Writing Paragraphs

A paragraph is a group of sentences all related to the same main idea. There are three components to a well-constructed paragraph: (1) main idea or topic sentence; (2) one or more sentences that explain, define, or provide details about and examples of the main idea; (3) conclusion. Figure 3.2 is a paragraph map showing the relationships among the sentences in a paragraph. Note the similarities and connections between Figures 3.1 and 3.2.

Before beginning to write a paragraph, use the map in Figure 3.2 to help you organize your ideas. You can also organize and gather your ideas by making a list or freewriting: writing

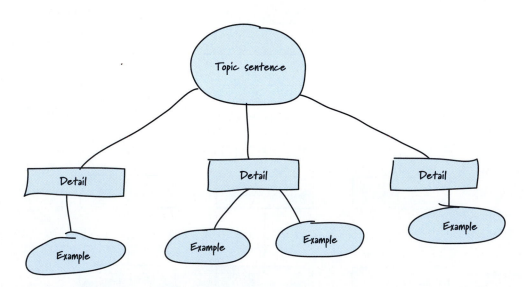

FIGURE 3.2   Paragraph Map

down everything you know and want to say about the topic and then selecting your best ideas to use in your paragraph. The ability to construct well-written, unified paragraphs will help you earn extra points on exams and assignments. But to earn those points, always remember to proofread what you have written. The proofreading checklist in Figure 3.3 will help you focus your attention.

___The topic sentence accurately reflects your most important point or main idea.

___The paragraph is unified because all of the sentences relate to your topic and topic sentence.

___The conclusion is an accurate reflection of the points made in your topic sentence and the body of your paragraph.

___The spelling, punctuation, capitalization, and usage in your paragraph are correct.

___The sentences in your paragraph are complete sentences, with no fragments, run-on sentences, or comma splices.

FIGURE **3.3**   **Paragraph Proofreading Checklist**

There are dozens of different types of paragraph writing assignments or short-answer exam questions you may encounter in your courses. The following are just a few examples of different types of paragraph assignments or short-answer exam questions, along with ideas of how to approach them:

Process direction paragraphs. Process direction paragraphs are analogous to the instructions included in the consumer goods you buy that require some assembly. Process direction paragraphs describe a stepwise process.

Someone reading a process direction paragraph you've written should be able to repeat the steps you've explained and duplicate the result of the process. Process direction paragraphs are common writing assignments in chemistry, physics, biology, and technology courses, where, after completing a lab, you may be required to write down the tasks you performed, in the order you performed them, and the results.

Process explanation paragraphs. Process explanation paragraphs explain a process that is not expected to be duplicated. In other words, process explanation paragraphs don't require your reader to do anything but understand the factors and variables that cause something to happen. Assignments in history, government, psychology, and business courses often require students to write process explanation paragraphs, to explain how a historical event, a political campaign, a psychological model, or a marketing plan, for example, worked in the past or might work in the future.

Classification paragraphs. In your reading about sensory, cognitive, and social learning preferences in this chapter, you've been reading classification paragraphs. Classification paragraphs divide larger generic groups of items into smaller groups of items that share certain characteristics. Consider students. You could classify all students by educational level: elementary school, middle school, high school, college, or graduate school. Or you might classify college students by their majors. Notice that the original group is broad, formed on the basis of a single criterion: all students or all college students.

The classification process divides that larger group by type. You will find yourself writing classification paragraphs often in assignments for a number of courses, including psychology courses (for example, the classification of various phobias and manias) and biology, chemistry, and geology courses (where the use of classification is integral to the field). Political science courses also require classification to distinguish among political ideologies, economic systems, and political parties.

Writing Essays

An essay is simply a series of paragraphs that relate to one idea, an idea expressed in a thesis statement. The elements of a basic essay include an introductory or lead-in paragraph with a thesis statement; three or more body paragraphs that explain and support the thesis statement; and a concluding paragraph. Table 3.2 compares the structure of a paragraph and an essay.

TABLE 3.2   Comparison of Structure: The Paragraph and the Essay

Structural Element	Paragraph	Essay
Topic	Topic sentence	Introductory paragraph and thesis statement
Supporting details	Body sentences	Body paragraphs
Conclusion	Concluding sentence	Concluding paragraph

Approach essay writing using the same list or freewriting techniques you use to write paragraphs. Then use the introductory paragraph to provide general background information, reasons, or rhetorical questions that lead to the thesis statement, which is the keystone that supports the ideas in your essay. The body paragraphs in your essay each contain a topic sentence that relates to the thesis statement. The topic sentences for the body paragraphs can be organized in spatial or time-sequence order or in order of importance:

Body paragraph 1: The most important reason is . . .

Body paragraph 2: Another reason is . . .

Body paragraph 3: The final reason is . . .

The conclusion paragraph of an essay, like the conclusion sentence of a paragraph, signals the end, summarizes the points made, and leaves the reader with a final thought or two about the implications of what you have written.

Once you have written an essay and are satisfied that you have included all of the elements, remember to spell check and grammar check your essay using the programs on your computer. Since these programs do not catch every mistake, you should proofread your final essay before you turn it in. Using a proofreading checklist, like the one in Figure 3.4, will help you focus on your proofreading.

___The introduction and thesis statement accurately reflect the topic and what you intend to describe in your essay.

___Each body paragraph has a topic sentence that relates to your thesis statement.

___The sentences in each body paragraph are unified and relate to the topic sentence of the paragraph.

___The order of your body paragraphs is logical, and your use of order—importance, spatial, time—is clear.

___There are appropriate transitions between and within paragraphs.

___The conclusion is an accurate reflection of the thesis statement and/or a final point you want your reader to contemplate.

___The spelling, punctuation, capitalization, and usage in your essay are correct.

___The sentences in your essay are complete sentences, with no fragments, run-on sentences, or comma splices.

FIGURE 3.4   **Essay Proofreading Checklist**

Have You Connected? Self-Assessment

After completing Chapter 3, answer the following questions about what you have learned:

1. What is your sensory learning preference: visual, auditory, or tactile? _____

2. What are your cognitive and social learning preferences? _____

   _____

3. Which online sites have you investigated to find out more about learning preference inventories? _____

   _____

4. What questions do you ask yourself when you are trying to find major and minor supporting details in a reading? _____

_____

_____

5. How are paragraphs and essays organized and written? _____

_____

_____

Chapter 3 Summary

Individual Learning Preferences

1. Sensory learning preferences explain how you receive information. The three types of learning preference are visual, auditory, and tactile.

2. Study strategies based on your visual, auditory, or tactile learning preferences can help you study more effectively.

3. Cognitive learning preferences describe how you process the information you receive. Four types of cognitive learning preferences are analytical, innovative, dynamic, and commonsense.

4. Your social learning preference indicates whether you study more effectively alone or with others.

5. Online surveys and inventories provide you with information about yourself as well as suggestions for study strategies.

Get Connected with Reading: Major and Minor Details

1. Details provide facts, statistics, dates, examples, reasons, steps, sequences, and any other information that is necessary to fully understand a topic.

2. Major details provide information about and direct support for the main idea. To identify major details, ask, "What else does the author want me to know about the main idea?"

3. Minor details explain and provide additional information about a major detail, not the main idea. To identify minor details, ask, "Does this detail support or explain a major detail instead of the main idea?"

Get Connected with Writing: Paragraphs and Essays

1. Paragraphs are groups of sentences all related to the same main idea or topic sentence. There are three components to well-written paragraphs: (1) the main idea or topic sentence; (2) one or more sentences that explain, define, or provide details about and examples of the main idea; (3) a conclusion.

2. Process paragraphs either describe a series of steps that can be followed to achieve an end result (direction) or explain more generally how something works (explanation), and

classification paragraphs are used to break down a large group into categories based on specific criteria.

3. An essay consists of a series of paragraphs that relate to one idea, an idea expressed in a thesis statement. The elements of a basic essay include an introductory or lead-in paragraph with a thesis statement; three or more body paragraphs that explain and support the thesis statement; and a concluding paragraph.

References

Diaz, David P., and Ryan B. Cartnal. 1999. "Comparing Student Learning Styles in an Online Distance Learning Class and an Equivalent On-Campus." *College Teaching* 47, no. 4: 130–135.

4 Thinking Critically

Critical thinking is the skill that takes you beyond memorizing and recalling facts from your textbook to pass exams. Critical thinking is the skill that moves you beyond basic comprehension and your ability to summarize and repeat what you've read in your textbook. Knowing facts and comprehending ideas are prerequisites to higher-level thinking, but knowledge and understanding are not themselves higher-level thinking skills. You must have command over the material before you can begin to think critically about it. The skills that critical thinking encompasses include being able to apply, analyze, synthesize, and evaluate what you have read, heard, seen, and experienced.

In this chapter, you will be exploring your thinking skills: critical, creative, and practical. You will also learn how to use critical reading skills to identify an author's tone, purpose, and intended audience and how to apply your critical thinking skills to write evaluative essays.

Are You Connected? Self-Assessment

Answer the following questions by circling Y for yes or N for no. Revisit this assessment after you have completed the chapter to see if any of your answers have changed.

Y   N   **1.** Do you know how to use strategies that will help you think critically?

Y   N   **2.** Do you know how to think creatively and use practical thinking skills to solve problems?

Y   N   **3.** Do you know how you can use technology to improve and practice your critical thinking skills?

Y   N   **4.** Can you explain what *tone, purpose,* and *intended audience* mean?

Y   N   **5.** Do you know how to write evaluative essays?

Learning Objectives

After completing Chapter 4, you should be able to demonstrate the following skills:

1. Understand critical thinking and the strategies that can help you become a critical thinker.

2. Understand creative thinking and how to use practical thinking to solve your academic, professional, and personal problems.

3. Understand and identify tone, purpose, and intended audience in your reading.

4. Understand the purpose and essential elements of evaluative essays.

Thinking Critically

When you read a textbook or listen to a lecture, you acquire information. But to use that information in meaningful ways, you must think critically about it. *Thinking critically* has to do with the questions you ask, the choices you make, and the reasoning you apply to what you learn. Thinking critically is also the process through which you come up with new ideas, approaches, and concepts, and find practical solutions to problems.

Critical thinking is a skill that enables you to identify and focus on the most important elements and concepts that you encounter in your studies, at work, and in your personal life. Your ability to think critically fuels your creativity, the source of new ideas and approaches to the challenges you face. Critical thinking also forms the basis of your problem-solving skills, the ability to find practical solutions to problems ranging from getting to school to choosing your major.

Bloom's Taxonomy of Learning and Thinking

You will be required to think critically in your college courses. To understand what this means and how your professors will encourage and evaluate your critical thinking, you must first consider the nature of thinking. In 1956, Benjamin Bloom developed a taxonomy (classification system) that identified six levels of learning and thinking (see Figure 4.1).

Knowledge   The first level of Bloom's taxonomy is knowledge. *Knowledge* involves reading your textbook and learning the facts and details there, or attending class and paying attention during lectures and then studying your notes to learn facts for your exams. Knowledge is what is being tested in true/false, multiple-choice, matching, and fill-in-the-blank questions on your exams. You have already learned several skills that are applicable to the knowledge level of thinking: using a reading and study system and understanding the clues that help you identify details in your reading assignments and lectures.

Comprehension   The second level in Bloom's taxonomy is *comprehension*—understanding what you read in your textbook and hear during lectures. Essay and short-answer exam questions that ask you to explain, relate, or summarize are aimed at testing your comprehension.

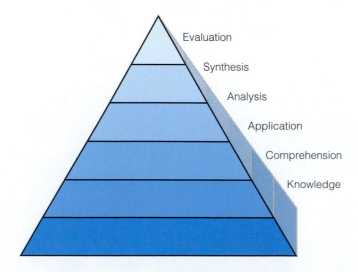

FIGURE **4.1**   **Bloom's Taxonomy of Learning and Thinking** *Source:* Bloom (1956)

Finding and formulating topics and writing about what you have read require the second level of thinking in Bloom's model.

Application   The third level of Bloom's taxonomy is *application,* the ability to take what you have learned in one situation and use it in other situations. For example, when you use the study strategies you've learned in this course in your history, literature, or psychology courses, you are applying knowledge you've learned in one situation to another situation. Essay and short-answer questions that prompt you to organize, demonstrate, describe, or apply understanding to another set of facts test your application skills.

Analysis   Bloom's fourth level of thinking is *analysis,* thinking about and looking for relationships in the material you have learned, comprehended, and applied. When you analyze, you make comparisons, determine cause and effect, or support and defend ideas, concepts, and principles—all skills that can be tested in essay and short-answer questions.

Synthesis   The fifth level of Bloom's taxonomy is *synthesis.* This level requires you to modify what you know to create new ideas or to make predictions. At this level of thinking, originality and creativity are key. Essay and short-answer questions that direct you to modify, design, create, or predict test your synthesis skills.

Evaluation   The final level of Bloom's model is *evaluation,* the ability to criticize, rate, and appraise the concepts you have learned. On the surface, it may seem that making a value judgment is easier than synthesizing information, but the reasoning required to justify your evaluations makes this level of thinking very challenging. Essay and short-answer exam questions that ask you to choose a side on an issue—usually for or against—and to justify your choice are testing your evaluation abilities.

Using Critical Thinking Skills

Critical thinking begins with a good foundation, doing a good job of acquiring information. This means reading your textbook assignments, attending all of your lectures and labs, and using your individual learning strategies (see Chapter 3) to help you focus on what you see, hear, and experience. Next, ask questions of yourself, your professor, and your classmates about what you are studying and learning. Write your comments, questions, and thoughts down in your notes or in the margins of your textbook. Asking questions—wondering what if, why, and how—is the first step in moving beyond knowledge and comprehension.

Practicing and applying what you learn in one course to other courses and to other situations will help you master the application level of thinking. For example, you can take what you have learned about goal setting, time management, and motivation in this course and apply it in your courses next semester or in your personal life. Application is using what you learn and know in other situations.

Once you have learned to adapt your skills to new circumstances, you are ready to progress to the analysis and synthesis levels of Bloom's thinking model. Each time you apply what you have learned to a new situation, remember to take the time to evaluate. When you evaluate, think about what worked well and what did not work well. You can then make adjustments the next time you need to apply your critical thinking skills in a similar situation.

Thinking critically is hard work. It takes more time and effort than just learning what is in your textbook and lecture notes. To think critically, you have to be willing to research what you do not know. And at times you have to admit that you cannot answer a question or resolve an issue. That frustration is a fact of life. If critical thinking were easy, if solutions were always obvious, there would be no war, no poverty, no disease, no hunger.

Also key to becoming a critical thinker is developing patience and tolerance for ideas that differ from the ones you hold. Although it can be difficult, try to understand viewpoints and opinions that are contrary to your own. Learn to withhold judgment, to pay attention to the words, not the feelings that the words arouse. Periodically summarizing what another person is saying—aloud or in writing—is a strategy that debaters, lawyers, and top sales executives use to stay focused on the issues instead of their emotions.

Finally, to become a critical thinker, you will have to subject yourself to risk. To analyze, synthesize, and evaluate, you may have to change the way you think and perceive. You may have to give up opinions and impressions that you have had for a long time, and you may find yourself thinking differently. Change can be frightening, and changing the way you view yourself and your beliefs and the beliefs of others can be particularly frightening. But the risks you take to become a critical thinker will pay off in the long run academically, professionally, and personally.

Get Connected with Critical Thinking

Answer the following questions about critical thinking. Circle the letter of the correct answer or write short responses in the spaces provided.

1. What are the six levels in Bloom's taxonomy of thinking, in order from first to last?

    a. Knowledge, comprehension, synthesis, analysis, application, and evaluation

    b. Knowledge, comprehension, application, synthesis, analysis, and evaluation

    c. Knowledge, application, comprehension, analysis, synthesis, and evaluation

    d. Knowledge, comprehension, application, analysis, synthesis, and evaluation

2. Which level of thinking did you rely on to answer question 1? _____

3. Which study strategies would you use to learn the information necessary to answer question 1? Why?

    Study strategies: _____

    Reasons chosen: _____

4. Compare and contrast the levels of skill necessary to progress from knowledge to evaluation in Bloom's taxonomy. _____

    _____

    _____

5. Which level of thinking did you rely on to answer question 4? _____

6. Summarize Bloom's taxonomy using your own words. _____

    _____

    _____

    _____

7. Which level of thinking did you rely on to answer question 6? _____

8. Critique Bloom's taxonomy as a tool or hierarchy for learning about critical thinking.

_____

_____

9. Which level of thinking did you rely on to answer question 8? _____

10. How can you use Bloom's taxonomy to help you prepare for your next exam? _____

_____

Creative Thinking

Creative thinking is often described as the ability to create something new by looking at the usual in imaginative ways. What does it take to think creatively? Certainly you have to be brave and not concerned with what other people think about you or your ideas. Think for a moment about how much courage some of the world's greatest explorers, inventors, and artists had, how much ridicule they initially endured because of their creativity. Have you ever considered how Michelangelo, Christopher Columbus, Benjamin Franklin, Wilbur and Orville Wright, Thomas Edison, Albert Einstein, and Howard Hughes were viewed by their contemporaries? A willingness to take risks is one characteristic creative thinkers share. Table 4.1 lists several others.

TABLE 4.1 **Common Characteristics of Creative Thinkers**

Characteristics	Behaviors
Willing to take risks	Try new ideas and concepts
Ignore limitations	Block out rules about the ways thing are done
Seek new challenges	Work on doing something better, easier, faster
Have broad interests	Interested in everything from art to science
Use old to create new	Want to improve what exists instead of reinventing it
Question status quo	Ask why it has to be done *this* way
Curious	Seek to understand how and why things work

Source: Schwartz (2005).

Creative thinking is not a totally separate type of thinking: It is a product of the synthesis level of critical thinking in Bloom's taxonomy. Creative thinking allows you to use what you have learned, understood, applied, and analyzed to come up with new and imaginative ideas. Not feeling very creative? To energize your creativity and boost your imagination, Brockman and Russell (2002) suggest the following strategies:

- Keep a journal, and write or draw whatever you are thinking about in it for ten minutes every day.

- Cut out pictures from magazines or newspapers, and arrange them creatively.

- Listen to soothing music or the sounds of nature while you close your eyes and contemplate.

- Play word games like crossword puzzles, word jumbles, or riddles; or play strategy games like chess or bridge.

- Ask "What if . . . ?" and then consider the possibilities.

Get Connected with Creative Thinking

Practice 1: Tangrams

A tangram is an ancient Chinese puzzle played with seven pieces, called *tans*. The object is to use the tans to create shapes. The pieces must be touching but not overlapping. Tangrams challenge you to think critically and creatively by asking you to use your spatial-visual, logical-mathematical, and bodily-kinesthetic intelligences to envision, organize, and manipulate the tans to create a whole from the seven random parts. Utah State University maintains a site (http://nlvm.usu.edu/en/nav/vm1_asid_112.html) where you can try your hand at tangrams. Visit the website and see if you can create the figures at the bottom of the screen. An example of a tangram is shown in Figure 4.2.

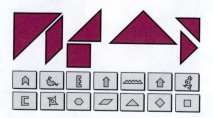

FIGURE 4.2 **Tangram** *Source:* National Library of Virtual Manipulatives for Interactive Mathematics, Utah State University (http://nlvm.usu.edu/en/nav/vm1_asid_112.html). Reprinted by permission.

Practice 2: Sudoku

A sudoku is a Japanese number puzzle consisting of a grid of eighty-one squares divided into nine blocks of nine squares each. The object of the game is to fill in the empty squares (some squares are already filled in) so that the numbers 1 through 9 appear only once in each row, column, and block (Emling 2005). Sudoku puzzles challenge you to recognize patterns and relationships and to apply logic in deciding which numbers belong in the open squares. To solve a sudoku, then, you have to think both critically and practically. See if you can fill in the missing numbers and solve the sudoku in Figure 4.3.

	9	5	2		8		7	
2								5
	8			4			2	
		2				8		7
1		5		7				3
5		3				1		
	5			2			6	
6								4
	3		9		6	5	1	

FIGURE 4.3   Sudoku Courtesy of www.sudoku-solver.com <http://www.sudoku-solver.com>. Reproduced by permission.

Practical Thinking

Practical thinking is problem solving, and it has a broad range of applications in your academic, professional, and personal life. You use problem solving when you decide what to major in, which courses to take next semester, or how to plan your time when you have an important paper due and a big exam scheduled the same day. You also use problem solving to make choices at work, and to decide which job offer to accept, which car to buy, or which apartment to lease. Whenever you have decisions to make, conflicts to resolve, or problems to solve, you are applying your practical thinking skills.

The following steps describe how the problem-solving process works and what you should be thinking about during each stage of the process (Liu and Bera 2005; "Problem-Based Learning," 2001):

Step 1. Isolate the problem or the issue.   In this step, you are looking for causes, not effects. For example, suppose your problem is that you have not selected your courses for next semester. The question to ask yourself is "Why not?" The cause of the problem helps define the solution. If your delay in choosing your courses has to do with not wanting to take a required course in math, clearly the solution has to do with motivating yourself. But if the delay is the result of an external factor—say, your boss has been slow to get you your work schedule for next semester—you are going to need a different solution.

Step 2. Analyze the problem or issue.   Consider, for example, the results of not selecting your courses for next semester. It may be that the classes you need or want to take will be closed, or that you will not be able to fit your required courses into your schedule. While you are analyzing the problem, think about any causes you overlooked in step 1. For example, do you really dislike math all that much, or are you responding to math the way some of your friends do?

Step 3. After isolating causes and effects, begin to brainstorm.   When you brainstorm, you think of all the possible solutions to your problem. You brainstorm for much the same

reasons that you freewrite or make a list as you prepare to write an essay. Your initial focus when you brainstorm is quantity, not quality. Write down everything you can think of that is related to the problem or issue you are trying to solve. You can evaluate your ideas later, after you gather your thoughts. To expand your list of ideas, you may want to brainstorm with a group of people.

Using analogies or similar situations is also a helpful brainstorming strategy. The problem you are trying to solve may be one that you have never experienced, but it also may be similar to an experience you have had. Think about what you did or decided then, and how your former experience relates to your current situation. Another good strategy to improve your brainstorming is to think about your problem or issue over a couple of days. Sometimes your best ideas come to you when you are doing something completely different later in the day or later in the week. Finally, when you are brainstorming, do not become obsessed with the solution, the right answer, or the best decision. If you focus on getting the right answer, you may close yourself off from considering the full range of possibilities.

Step 4. Evaluate each possible solution.   In this step, consider the pluses and minuses of each alternative. This is the stage at which you eliminate ideas that are not practical, that are more negative than positive, or that are just bad ideas.

Step 5. Select the best, most reasonable, and most complete solution, and implement it.   If, for example, you decide that you should visit the counseling center to discuss your concerns and course selections before you register for next semester, set up a plan for yourself. To implement your solution, decide when you will go to the counseling center and what questions you will ask.

Step 6. Evaluate the solution you chose.   After you implement your solution and resolve your course selection issues, for example, think about how the solution worked. Start by asking these questions:

- Did you choose a good solution? If not, what was wrong with the choice you made?
- If this type of problem or issue arises again, would you choose the same or a similar solution? If not, what would you do instead?

Step 7. Make changes to improve your critical thinking process and the way you solved this problem.   This step helps prepare you for the next problem you face. You will know what you should and should not use to solve the same or a similar problem in the future.

Get Connected with Practical Thinking

Practice 1: Problem Solving

Assume that you have not yet decided on your college major. In the spaces below, note how you would use the problem-solving process to reach a decision. Your school's online catalog, which lists degree and certificate programs, may be a good resource to help you brainstorm.

1. Isolate the problem: _____

2. Analyze the problem: _____

3. Brainstorm possible solutions: _____

_____

4. Evaluate the pros and cons of your brainstorming solutions: _____

_____

5. Select the best solution and implement it: _____

6. Evaluate the solution: _____

_____

7. Make changes to improve the process: _____

_____

Get Connected with Technology: Sharpen Your Thinking Skills Online

There are many sites on the Internet that will challenge you and help you improve your critical, creative, and practical thinking skills. The following are some examples for you to explore:

- Maricopa Community Colleges maintain a site where you can apply your problem solving skills to buying a car (http://www.mcli.dist.maricopa.edu/pbl/ubuystudent/process.html).
- Visit Chess Is Fun (http://www.princeton.edu/~jedwards/cif/chess.html) to play chess with the United States Correspondence Chess Champion.
- The American Contract Bridge League home page (http://www.acbl.org) has information on learning to play bridge.
- You can do the crossword of the day or test yourself on trivia at Quizland (http://quizland.com); there are jigsaw puzzles and card games at GoToFreeGames.com.
- At How Stuff Works (http://www.howstuffworks.com), you can see exactly how engines, electronics, computers, and the Internet work.

Game playing calls on the skills that make higher levels of thought possible. The Internet offers a seemingly endless supply of problem-solving and creative thinking games that will help you exercise and improve your critical, creative, and practical thinking skills.

Get Connected with Reading: Tone, Purpose, and Intended Audience

To think critically about what you read, you must go beyond the words in the text to analyze and discover deeper meaning. Reading to identify the topic, main-idea sentence, and supporting details in a paragraph is a skill that is necessary to succeed in your courses; it is also necessary to achieve the knowledge and comprehension levels in Bloom's taxonomy. However, to reach the higher levels of thinking, you will need higher-level reading skills. Specifically, you must be able not only to read, understand, and comprehend, but also to think about the text and determine the author's tone, purpose, and intended audience: How does the author feel about the topic? Why is the author writing on the subject? Who is the author's audience?

Tone

Tone can be described as the author's voice: It reflects how the author feels about what he or she has written about. Tone, in other words, is attitude. When you speak, it is very easy to determine your attitude from your inflection. Your voice changes when you are angry, happy, serious, cynical, or ambivalent. When you are reading an assignment, pay attention to the words the author chooses to discuss the subject matter. Word choice indicates the author's attitude about the topic.

As you read, be aware of the descriptive language the author uses and the positive or negative impressions the words convey. When you are trying to identify tone, consider the author's word choice and ask yourself: "What is the author's attitude toward the subject matter?" The adjectives that can be used to describe tone are as many and varied as the vocabulary words you know that express emotions. An author's tone varies depending on the author's purpose and audience, and the type of publication. In the pages of a newspaper, for example, you would find the objective tone of the reporters covering news stories, and the more subjective tone of columnists and readers (in letters to the editor), who are expressing their opinions. And, of course, there is the tone used by editorial cartoonists, a broad application of humor, often with a large dose of irony or satire.

Stories of war—like the work of Nobel Prize–winning author Elie Wiesel, who wrote of his experiences in the Holocaust—often convey a sense of tragedy, and they often shock the reader. Articles and stories about modern Africa, of genocide in Rwanda and Sudan, starvation in Ethiopia, and AIDS in South Africa, also convey tragedy. But in these stories the reader is likely to find indignation, too, anger that no one is taking or has taken action to stop the murder, the hunger, or the disease.

The tone of authors who write romance novels or articles for lifestyle magazine tends to be optimistic, occasionally nostalgic or even melancholy. People who write human-interest stories make use of emotion as part of their craft, and the various tones that evoke emotion are integral to the genre.

Textbook authors, on the other hand, tend to be objective. The purpose of a textbook is to inform and instruct. Therefore, textbook authors usually focus on the pertinent facts with minimal commentary. But you will find a wide variety of tones in assigned readings in your literature and journalism courses and, of course, in your research materials.

Being able to determine an author's tone can help you evaluate what the author is "saying." The author's attitude about the subject matter also affects the credibility of the information the author is presenting. That is, the author's tone can help you determine a bias or a motive that calls the information into question and points out the need to look for alternate sources on the same subject.

Purpose

Purpose explains why an author wrote a text. Authors write for a number of reasons. For example, a cookbook author writes to inform readers. The author of a textbook generally writes for the purpose of instruction, to explain concepts and processes in a specific field of study. A newspaper editor may write an editorial to persuade readers to take action—to vote for or against a candidate or a ballot measure, or to get involved in community affairs. Advertising copywriters also write to persuade readers, in this case to buy a product or service. Gossip columnists write to entertain readers. Other journalists do investigative reporting. To inform, to instruct, to persuade, to entertain, and to investigate are among the most common reasons authors have for writing.

Understanding the author's purpose puts you in a better position to evaluate and analyze what you have read. For example, if you know that the author has written the text to persuade readers, you will be aware that the author may have omitted certain facts or information that does not support the position he or she is promoting. Often authors who write editorials, columns, or commercial copy are selective about what material they include and omit. Being a critical reader means determining the author's purpose and then evaluating the validity of the information in light of that purpose; it also means searching for other sources on the same subject to be sure that you have all of the information and facts on both sides of an issue so that you can make an informed decision about or judgment on that issue.

To determine what the author's purpose is for writing a particular passage, read the entire selection, and then ask yourself, "Why did the author write this text?" Although most authors do not tell the reader directly why they wrote a particular passage, the text itself sometimes provides clues to help you determine the author's purpose.

Intended Audience

The *intended audience* is the group of people for whom the author is writing. The intended audience can be broad—adults in the general public, children in elementary or middle school, high school or college students—or narrow—cardiologists, estate lawyers, civil engineers. Authors adjust their vocabulary, the use of technical terminology, the level of writing, and the depth of coverage to fit their intended audience.

To determine the author's intended audience, read the passage carefully and then ask yourself, "Which readers is the author addressing?" Some authors specify their intended audience. Textbook authors, for example, write for students at certain levels, ranging from elementary school through graduate school. Authors who write for law journals, medical journals, or technical trade journals also have an intended audience in mind when they choose topics and make word choices. The same is true of the people who write for teen magazines, say, or other specialty publications. Even the reporters and editors of newspapers and general-circulation magazines, which target a much broader audience, choose topics and vocabulary suitable for their readers.

When trying to determine an author's intended audience, look at the topic of the writing. Is the topic simple or complex? The more complex and technical the topic, the more sophisticated the intended audience. Another clue to intended audience is the vocabulary in the piece. Is the vocabulary basic or specialized? The more technical the vocabulary, the more sophisticated the intended audience.

Get Connected with Writing: Evaluative Essays

When you write an evaluative essay, you examine and make value judgments about the subject matter of your essay. Remember that evaluation is the highest level of thinking in Bloom's taxonomy.

You come across written evaluations every day. Every time you read a review of a concert, a play, a film, or a book, you are reading evaluative writing. When you agree with the reviewer, chances are you think that the review is comprehensive, fair, and accurate. When you disagree, you may insist that the reviewer is being too critical, that the review is neither fair nor accurate. Your knowledge and experience with evaluative formats and your understanding of the use of tone to convey positive and negative attitudes will help you when you write evaluative essays; so will your remembering the positive and negative reviews you have read and your reactions to them.

In your college courses, you will be required to write evaluative essays on literature, psychological studies, scientific methods, and historical or political events. You may find slight differences in individual assignments. For example, one might ask you to express your values, while another asks you to write a *referential evaluative essay,* an essay in which you describe how several reliable authorities evaluate your topic. Or you may be asked to incorporate persuasion, to make a convincing argument that your judgment on the subject is correct and should be adopted. Whatever the differences, there are three basic components you must include in every evaluative essay:

- The story or a description of the subject matter you are going to evaluate
- Your judgment, what you think about the subject matter
- Standards or criteria that support your judgment

Although these components are described as single paragraphs—the model essay consists of five paragraphs: introduction and thesis statement, three body paragraphs, and a concluding paragraph—evaluative essays can be structured differently and can be much longer and more detailed than the model.

Subject Matter. The subject matter of an evaluative essay can be presented as narration or description. In other words, you can write your subject-matter paragraph as a story or as a description. Remember, though, that the description in your evaluative essay should be short. Your purpose here is not to describe a person or place in detail but to provide enough information and detail so that your value judgment on the subject matter will make sense.

Your Judgment. In this paragraph of your evaluative essay, you write your position or stand on the subject matter. Know that your judgment can be positive or negative or both. But if you choose to highlight both good and bad, you will have to make a decision on whether the good points outweigh the bad points in your overall evaluation.

Standards or Criteria. Standards, or criteria, are the measures you use in making your judgment, the basis of your decision. For a judgment to be credible, it must be based on meaningful criteria. That is, the criteria you use should be the same or equivalent to the criteria that would be applied to subjects similar to yours.

Have You Connected? Self-Assessment

After completing Chapter 4, answer the following questions about what you have learned:

1. What strategies have you learned that will help you think critically and creatively?

   _____

2. What are the seven steps in the problem-solving process?

   Step 1: _____

   Step 2: _____

   Step 3: _____

   Step 4: _____

   Step 5: _____

   Step 6: _____

   Step 7: _____

3. Which websites have you visited and what types of games, puzzles, and exercises have you used to practice improving your critical thinking skills?

   _____

   _____

4. What do *tone, purpose,* and *intended audience* mean?

   Tone: _____

   Purpose: _____

   Intended audience: _____

5. What is an evaluative essay? _____

   _____

Chapter 4 Summary
Thinking Critically

1. Thinking can be classified as critical, creative, and practical.
2. Critical thinking involves multiple levels of thinking difficulty, from knowledge and comprehension to application, analysis, synthesis, and evaluation.

3. Creative thinking lets you use your imagination and synthesis skills to develop new ideas.

4. Practical thinking, or problem solving, helps you make the best decisions.

5. The problem-solving process involves seven steps: (1) isolate the issue, (2) analyze, (3) brainstorm, (4) weigh the potential solutions, (5) choose the best solution, (6) evaluate the process, and (7) make changes to improve the process.

6. The web is a wonderful source of games, puzzles, and exercises to help you practice and develop your critical thinking skills.

Get Connected with Reading: Tone, Purpose, and Intended Audience

1. Tone is the author's attitude toward the subject matter; it generally is reflected in the author's choice of words.

2. Purpose explains why the author wrote the text; it is an important factor in determining the credibility of the information there.

3. Intended audience refers to the people the author expects to read the text; it generally is reflected in both the subject matter and the vocabulary of the material.

Get Connected with Writing: Evaluative Essays

1. Evaluative essays are used to make value judgments about a particular subject matter.

2. Evaluative essays include three essential elements: a narration or description of the subject matter, the judgment, and the criteria used to make the judgment.

References

Bloom, Benjamin S. 1956. *A Taxonomy of Educational Objectives. Handbook 2, The Cognitive Domain.* New York: Longman.

Brockman, Michael S., and Stephen T. Russell. 2002. "Creativity." National 4-H Council and the University of Arizona. http://msg.calsnet.arizona.edu/fcs/content.cfm?content5creativity (accessed August 18, 2005).

Emling, Shelley. 2005. "Here's a Puzzle to Tickle Your Mind." *Austin American-Statesman,* May 20.

Liu, Min, and Stephan Bera. 2005. "An Analysis of Cognitive Tool Use Patterns in a Hypermedia Learning Environment." *Educational Technology Research & Development* 53, no. 1: 5–21.

National Library of Virtual Manipulatives for Interactive Mathematics, Utah State University. http://nlvm.usu.edu/en/nav/vm1_asid_112.html (accessed August 25, 2005).

"Problem-Based Learning." 2001. Maricopa Center for Learning & Instruction, Maricopa Community Colleges. http://www.mcli.dist.maricopa.edu/pbl/ubuystudent/process.html, September 26 (accessed August 18, 2005).

Schwartz, Wendy. 2005. "Strategies for Identifying the Talents of Diverse Students." Idaho's Gifted and Talented. http://www.sde.state.id.us/GiftedTalented/Biblio/showone.asp?iId515 (accessed August 18, 2005).

"Sudoku Solver." 2005. Deadman's Handle. www.sudoku-solver.com (accessed August 3, 2005).

5

Taking Textbook and Lecture Notes

You probably have developed your own unique method and style for taking notes on reading assignments and class lectures, and your method and style probably have worked for you until now. But note taking is an essential skill in college. Without good notes on your textbook readings and on lectures, you will not have the necessary information to study and review so you can master what you need to know and understand . . . and do well on your exams.

An understanding of how the material in your textbook and in your professors' lectures is organized can help you take better notes. Recognizing the format a textbook author or a professor is using can help you anticipate the order of the presentation, predict what will come next, and take notes more efficiently. Using those same patterns of organization when you read and write can help you complete your assignments, learn classroom material, and respond to essay exam questions more effectively.

Are You Connected? Self-Assessment

Answer the following questions by circling Y for yes and N for no. Revisit this assessment after you have completed the chapter to see if any of your answers have changed.

Y   N   **1.** Do you know at least three different ways to take textbook notes?

Y   N   **2.** Do you know at least five strategies that will help you take better lecture notes?

Y   N   **3.** Do you know how you can use technology to help you with your textbook and lecture notes?

Y   N   **4.** Do you know the clues that can help you identify patterns of organization?

Y   N   **5.** Do you know how to write using patterns of organization?

Learning Objectives

After completing Chapter 5, you should be able to demonstrate the following skills:

1. Understand the forms, formats, and strategies you can use to take effective textbook and lecture notes.

2. Know how to use technology to help you prepare, organize, and master essential note-taking skills.

3. Identify definition, sequence, list, compare-contrast, and cause-and-effect patterns of organization when you see or hear them in your assigned readings and lectures.

4. Write your textbook and lecture notes, paragraphs, and essays using patterns of organization.

Essential Note-Taking Skills

One of the skills you need to excel at in college is note taking. Over the course of your college experience, you will take thousands of pages of notes on what you read in your textbooks and on what you see, hear, and do in lectures, labs, and discussion groups. Clearly, efficient note taking is an invaluable skill. So is effective note taking: You will need accurate and complete notes to finish assignments, write papers, and study for exams. Your course grades will reflect just how effective your note-taking skills are.

Essentially, you will be taking two main types of notes in college: on textbook assignments and on lectures. You will use the notes on your textbook to prepare for lectures; to review, rehearse, and master the material in your textbook; and to study for exams. Taking notes on textbook materials in general is easier than taking lecture notes because you are not under as much pressure. You can pace your textbook note taking as you read, stopping to think about what you want to include in your notes and how you want to write it. Lecture notes, on the other hand, are taken during live presentations. Your time to pause and reflect about the information presented is limited by how fast your professor is speaking and how quickly you can write.

Taking Textbook Notes

Before you go to a lecture, you should complete the reading assignment your professor will be discussing. Look to your course syllabus for reading assignments and lecture topics so you will know how to prepare and what to expect. If you read and make notes on your assignment before class, you will find that you do not have to work as hard during class—that you do not have to try to write down everything your professor says. Instead, you can focus on information to enhance your existing notes, the explanations and interpretations your professor makes that are not in the textbook.

The notes you take on your textbook readings should be based on your reading and study system (see Chapter 1). You should be using PQR or a reading and study system you have developed yourself. In other words, you should start by previewing the assigned material, and then ask yourself questions as you read, answer those questions as you read, and make notes; you should also review your textbook notes when you complete the assignment.

There are many ways to make notes on your reading assignments. Among the most widely used methods are the following:

- Highlighting
- Annotating
- Outlining
- Mind mapping
- Divided-page note taking

Each of these methods has certain strengths and weaknesses. The choices you make from this list should vary depending on the nature of the material you are reading. That is, your notes on readings for a math or biology course should be organized and written differently from the notes you make on readings for a literature or history course. In addition, these different methods of taking textbook notes are not mutually exclusive. You can use several different methods to complete a single reading assignment. For example, you may decide to make notes in your textbook as you read (annotation) and also create mind maps for certain material in the assigned reading.

Your objective in this section is not only to understand the choices available to you for taking notes on what you read, but also to find or develop methods that work for you. When it is time to choose one or more methods of taking textbook notes, think about your learning preferences (see Chapter 3), the way the textbook is organized, the types of information you need to master in the textbook, and what appeals to you about each of the note-taking strategies.

Highlighting

Using highlighters to mark textbooks is popular because the process is quick and easy. Choosing different colors is fun, and text marked with highlighting is easy to spot when you open your book. And then there's the convenience: You don't have to drag notebooks, paper, pens, or a laptop around campus; all you need is your text and your highlighter.

One important advantage of highlighting is that it helps you concentrate on the text you are reading because you will have to mark the text with your highlighter when you finish each section. Another advantage is your ability to color-code the text for easy reference—to use different colors to mark different types of information. You might decide, for example, to highlight main ideas in yellow, major details or key terms in blue, examples in green, and conclusions in orange.

One problem is deciding what to highlight. Too little, and you may neglect important information; too much, and the method loses its effectiveness. (If everything is highlighted, then nothing is!) A good rule of thumb is to highlight no more than 20 to 25 percent of the text you read. Your focus should be on key phrases. Another disadvantage of highlighting is that you can't use a highlighter to record your thoughts, reflections, comments, or questions about the text you are reading. That can lead to yet another difficulty: In the absence of notes, you may not remember why you chose to highlight certain terms, examples, or ideas instead

of others. Finally, if you want to sell your books at the end of the semester, you may not be able to find a buyer for a textbook that is heavily highlighted.

Annotating

Annotating is another way to take textbook notes. When you annotate, you read with a pencil in your hand, marking important points in the text and writing notes in the margins. For example, you might draw double lines under main points, draw single lines under major details, circle words you do not know, and make rectangles around key terms. Your marginal notes might be comments or reflections on the text, or numbers that indicate examples, lists, or steps embedded in the text.

One advantage of annotation is that it clarifies what you need to do—look up words you don't know in the glossary or a dictionary, and review and learn key terms, for example. Your marginal notes also give you a record of your thoughts that complements what you have marked in the text. Numbers or symbols—to show sequence or important phrases or concepts that you must know—add to the utility of your marginal notes, a flexibility that is missing from highlighting. Finally, because you annotate in pencil, it's a simple matter to erase a marking or a note if you make a mistake.

The biggest drawback to annotation is the size of the margins in most textbooks: You simply may not have enough room in the margins to note all the important points in the text that you want to remember. Crowded margins can also make it difficult to see and use your notes.

Outlining

Outlining is another method of taking notes on your textbook readings. It is a particularly good choice for political science, history, and sociology courses, which are all reading-based courses; it is less effective in math and science courses because of the way textbooks in those courses are organized.

You can outline informally, using indention to show relationships among main ideas, major and minor details, and examples. Or you can use a formal outline, a precise system of numbering, lettering, and indention to show relationships and degrees of importance:

- Main ideas are identified with roman numerals (I, II, III, . . .) and are positioned flush to the left margin.

- Major details are identified with capital letters (A, B, C, . . .) and are indented one unit from the left.

- Minor details are identified with Arabic numbers (1, 2, 3, . . .) and are indented two units from the left.

- Examples of minor details are identified with lowercase letters (a, b, c, . . .) and are indented three units from the left.

Figure 5.1 shows a formal outline of the first part of this chapter broken down by element.

Formal outline format:

I. Main idea
   A. Major detail
     1. Minor detail
     2. Minor detail
     3. Minor detail
     4. Minor detail
     5. Minor detail
       a. Example
       b. Example

Sample formal outline:

Essential note-taking skills
   Taking textbook notes
     Highlighting
     Annotating
     Outlining
     Mind mapping
     Divided-page note taki
       Two-column methoc
       Three-column meth

FIGURE 5.1   Formal Outline

Although formal outlines may look complicated, actually they are not. Many textbooks can easily be converted into formal outlines for note taking by using the chapter headings and subheadings as your outline entries. The outline on the right in Figure 5.1, for example, reflects the headings and subheadings in this section of Chapter 5. To determine the level of headings and subheadings in a textbook, look at the position of the heading and the font size and style (bold or italic). Usually, centered headings are more important than headings aligned at the left, and freestanding headings are more important than headings that run into the text. Also, the larger and bolder the font, the more important the heading. If you have difficulty telling the difference between major and minor points in a textbook, look at the chapter headings and subheadings in the table of contents. Often you can use the headings there as a basis for your formal outline, filling in minor headings as you read each section of the text. If you decide to copy a table of contents and use it as the basis of an outline for note taking, be sure to leave space between the headings and subheadings so you can add notes as you read each chapter.

Mind Mapping

Mind maps are graphic representations of information and ideas and of the relationships between and among them. Mind mapping helps you organize and visualize information, two processes that help you remember that information better. When you create a mind map, you visualize the text, using your imagination to think about the text, and draw connections that you might otherwise overlook. Mind mapping is a graphic form of summarizing: It requires you to understand what you are reading—the ideas, the details, and the relationships among them—and then to "rewrite" the text concisely, in words, images, and symbols of your own.

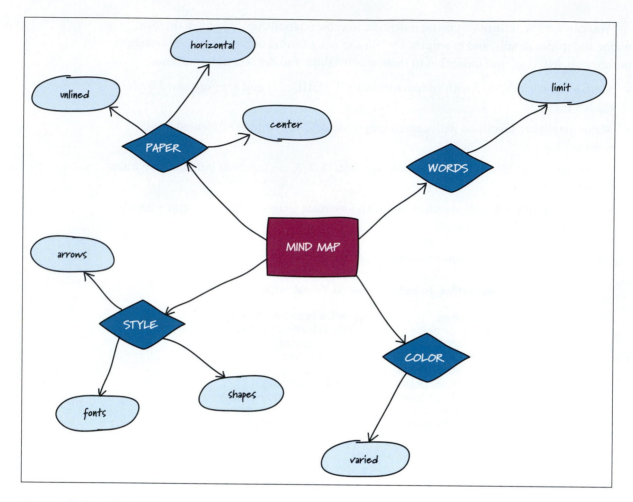

FIGURE 5.2 **Mind Map**

Mind mapping is also fun, which can motivate you to finish your reading assignments so you can start drawing or producing your maps by hand or on the computer.

As interesting, creative, and engaging as mind mapping is, there are several disadvantages to using it as your primary method for taking notes on readings. First, to show all the connections you find in a reading assignment, you may have to make several maps. The fun of making maps can wane quickly if you discover that you have to create four or five maps for every chapter of a fifteen-chapter textbook. When mapping becomes drudgery, the quality of the maps tends to go down, and so does the value of mind mapping as a review and study tool. In addition, mind mapping does not fit well with all textbook reading assignments.

Instead of choosing mind mapping as your primary note-taking method, consider using it whenever you need extra help to remember the relationships between elements—the branches of government, for example, or historical events. It's also a good tool to use now and again to add variety to your note taking.

Divided-Page Note Taking

To make use of divided-page note-taking systems, you divide the paper you use to take your notes into columns to simplify the process of reviewing your notes later, when you are studying for exams. You can use two or three columns, leaving space at the bottom of each page for a summary or comments.

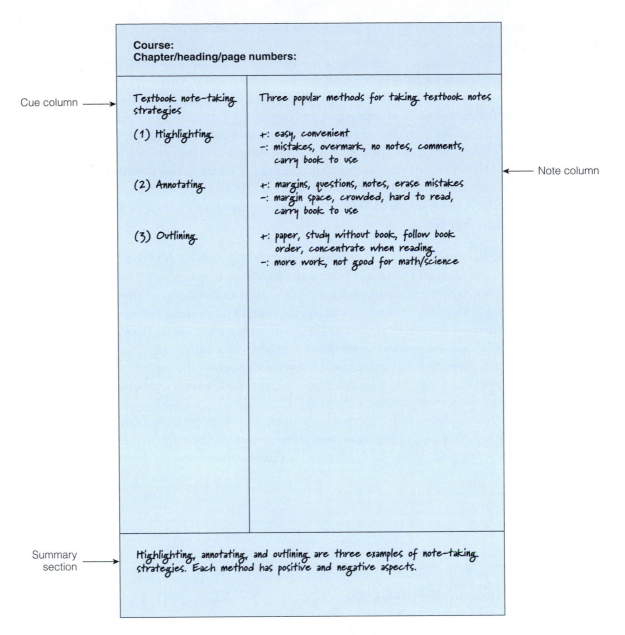

Cue column →

Note column ←

Summary section →

Course:
Chapter/heading/page numbers:

Textbook note-taking strategies

(1) Highlighting

(2) Annotating

(3) Outlining

Three popular methods for taking textbook notes

+: easy, convenient
−: mistakes, overmark, no notes, comments, carry book to use

+: margins, questions, notes, erase mistakes
−: margin space, crowded, hard to read, carry book to use

+: paper, study without book, follow book order, concentrate when reading
−: more work, not good for math/science

Highlighting, annotating, and outlining are three examples of note-taking strategies. Each method has positive and negative aspects.

FIGURE 5.3   Divided-Page Note Taking: Two-Column Format

Two-Column Method.   The Cornell System is one of the most common two-column methods; it has been used by generations of college students to take notes on readings and in lectures. The system uses a divided page to help you make connections between key concepts and the explanations, examples, and applications of those concepts.

To take Cornell System notes on a reading assignment, start with a blank sheet of paper—lined or unlined—and write the course name and the assignment at the top of the page. (For lecture notes, add the date to the first line, and replace the assignment with the lecture title.) Then create the two columns by drawing a vertical line down the paper, stopping about four-fifths of the way down (Figure 5.3). Position the vertical line so that the space to the left of it is roughly a third of the width of the page.

The cue column (left-hand column) is reserved for key terms, concepts, and principles, so the entries here should be short. By limiting the writing in the cue column to words and phrases, you will find it easy to scan your notes and locate a particular term, concept, or principle.

The note column on the right side of the page is for taking detailed notes, copying down examples, making lists, recording dates, and including any other facts that explain the key concepts in the cue column. You may find it more effective to start your note taking using only the right column of your paper, and to wait until you finish your reading assignment and review what you have written before filling in the cue column with key concepts.

You can use the summary section at the bottom of the page to condense and synthesize what you have written in your notes on the page. You may decide to write a summary when you finish a section of the text instead of doing a summary for each page of notes. Alternatively, you may decide to hold off writing a summary until later, when you review and rehearse your notes.

Three-Column Method.   Three-column note taking adds a third column. The method is used most often for taking notes on math and science textbook assignments and lecture and lab notes, to help you distinguish among key terms and concepts, examples, and rules or formulas. The three-column format can also include a summary section at the bottom of each page that can be used to synthesize the processes and formulas on the page or for later review and rehearsal. Because of the volume of numbers, equations, symbols, and calculations used in math, chemistry, and physics courses, you may discover that unless you clearly distinguish and label the material in your notes, you may not recall exactly what you did or how you did it when you review your notes (Nolting 2002).

Here, too, begin with a blank sheet of paper, and write the course name and the assignment at the top of the page. Then create your three columns by drawing two vertical lines, evenly spaced, down the paper. An example of the three-column format is shown in Figure 5.4.

Course: Chapter/heading/page numbers:		
Key terms	Examples	Rules/Formulas
Summary:		

FIGURE **5.4**   **Divided-Page Note Taking: Three-Column Format**

Strengths and weaknesses of the various methods of textbook note taking are summarized in Table 5.1.

TABLE 5.1   A Comparison of Note-Taking Methods

Method	Strengths	Weaknesses
Highlighting	Easy, use of color	Overmarking, mistakes, no comments or notes
Annotating	Comments, notes, easy to correct	Small margins, hard to read
Outlining	Easy to carry, based on headings	Not appropriate for math or science
Mind mapping	Connections and relationships	Labor intensive
Divided-page note taking		
Two column	Organized cues, notes, summaries	Lots of writing or typing
Three column	Key terms, examples, formulas	Not suitable for all material

Taking Lecture Notes

Many of the methods available to you for taking textbook notes can also be used to take lecture notes. You can outline, draw a mind map, or divide your notebook pages into two or three columns. Although there is something to be said for consistency in the methods you use to take notes on readings and lectures, ultimately the choices you make when you take lecture notes will be based on speed. Your professors speak much faster than you can write, so in lectures you do not have the luxury of deliberating over note-taking methods. You have to focus on getting all of the pertinent information down.

Some students use laptop computers and key in notes during lectures. Others use paper and pens. A pen is generally a better choice than a pencil because it is easier to write quickly with a pen. However, you might not need to write as quickly and you might be more comfortable using a pencil in math, science, or lab courses. Your choice of format and form will vary depending on the subject matter, the professor, and the purpose of your notes.

There are certain guidelines to keep in mind when you take lecture notes. In general, you must be alert, listen carefully, write quickly, and stay focused. Here are a number of specific strategies you can use when you take lecture notes. If you are not already using them, try one or more of them in the next lecture you attend.

Be ready as soon as the lecture starts.   Professors generally begin a lecture with an overview that can help you organize your thoughts, and you don't want to miss it. If you're using a divided-page method for taking notes, prepare your note paper (write the date, course title, and lecture or lab title at the top, and draw your vertical lines). If you take notes on a laptop, have a new document open and named and ready to go in your word-processing program. You want to be focused on listening as soon as the lecture or lab begins.

Focus on making a written record of the lecture.   Concentrate on what your professor is saying.

Don't waste time.   Don't take notes on material that is covered in your textbook and needs no further explanation.

Listen for the main ideas.   Your professors may directly state important ideas by using phrases like "First, I'm going to discuss . . . " or "Next, we will focus on . . . " They may also use pauses, gestures, or repetition to indicate the main ideas in a lecture.

Listen for clues to details.   Listen especially for numbers: "There are *four* important points . . . " or "The *three* main reasons are . . . " Then listen carefully for each of those points or reasons.

Copy down graphic aids.   If your professor doesn't hand out copies of graphic materials or make them available on a website, copy down whatever he or she puts on the board or projects on a screen.

Write down just one or two of the examples used to illustrate principles or main ideas.   Focus on one or two examples. In a math course, writing every problem down as an example is not necessary and may be more confusing than noting one or two problems and being sure they are clearly explained with formulas, rules, and processes.

Mark information that your professor says is important or difficult, or that may be on an exam.   Use stars or arrows, a colored pen or highlighter, or capital letters to indicate the information is important.

Don't stop taking notes until the lecture is over.   Most professors spend the last few minutes of a lecture summarizing what has been covered and previewing the next lecture, so that you know what to expect and how to prepare.

Define terms that are not defined in your textbook.   Make notes on new terms or synonyms for terms used in your textbook that your professor uses during the lecture. Include examples, explanations, and cross-references to your text that will help you make connections later, when you review your notes and use them to study for exams.

Leave a space between entries so that you can fill in missing information.   Always review your notes after class for accuracy. If something isn't clear, find out what you missed and add it to your notes. Your notes will be better, and the review is an opportunity to rehearse the information and begin learning it.

Develop a system of symbols, abbreviations, acronyms, and other shorthand techniques to help you keep up.   Using digits for dates (7/4/1776) instead of words (July 4, 1776) saves time. So does omitting vowels (*rdng* for "reading") and using symbols ($, #, &) and standard abbreviations (Jan., lb., CA). Make up your own abbreviations to save even more time. If your abbreviations are unusual or you think you might forget their meanings, add a key to your notes.

When the lecture is over, number the pages of your notes and review your notes as soon as possible. Remember that you forget as much as 50 percent of what you hear in a lecture shortly after the lecture is over. When you review your notes, fill in any missing information and make sure you understand (and can read!) what you wrote. Add any additional information you can think of to clarify your notes and make them more useful later, when it's time to review and master the material.

Get Connected with Lecture Note Taking

After taking a set of lecture notes using these strategies, complete the following assessment. Look carefully at your notes, and answer the following questions by circling Y for yes and N for no.

Y   N   **1.** Did you take time before class to prepare your note paper, or to open and name a new document in your word-processing program?

Y   N   **2.** Did you listen and watch for clues to the main ideas?

Y   N   **3.** Did you list the points your professor identified using numbers?

Y   N   **4.** Did you copy down graphic aids?

Y   N   **5.** Did you use symbols to indicate important points?

Y   N   **6.** Did you define new terms in your notes?

Y   N   **7.** Did you skip lines and leave space to add information later?

Y   N   **8.** Did you use abbreviations?

Y   N   **9.** Did you number the pages of your notes?

Y   N   **10.** Did you review your notes and fill in as much information as possible while the material was still fresh in your mind?

Give yourself 10 points for each Y answer and 0 points for each N answer. What is your score?

If your score is 70 or below, review the note-taking guidelines in this section again and work on incorporating them into your note taking during your next lecture class.

Get Connected with Technology: Online Note-Taking Tips

A good place to start a search for note-taking tips and tutorials online is your school's website. Many college-sponsored sites offer help with note taking, outlining, and mind mapping before, during, and after lectures. Here are just a few of them:

- For examples of the differences between highlighting too much and too little, try Mount Royal College's website (http://mtroyal.ab.ca/learningskills/study_studying .shtml).

- For information about the Cornell System and editing your notes, try Virginia Polytechnic Institute and State University's website (http://www.ucc.vt.edu/stdysk/stdyhlp.html).
- On its website (http://www.sarc.sdes.ucf.edu/studyhandouts.html), the Student Academic Resource Center of the University of Central Florida offers tips on and examples of outlines, patterns of organization, mind maps, and the Cornell format.

Get Connected with Reading: Identifying Patterns of Organization

Patterns of organization are the conventions that authors and lecturers use to present information. In other words, patterns of organization are the way authors and lecturers think about and organize the information in their written and oral presentations. You are already familiar with patterns of organization because you use them when you think, speak, and write. Of course, the way you organize and take notes on readings or lectures reflects the patterns of organization that the textbook author or your professor uses. When you review and study your notes, you can reorganize the information using a pattern that makes more sense to you. There are five common patterns of organization—definition, sequence, list, compare-contrast, and cause-and-effect—and they almost always are used in combination.

Definition Pattern

Authors use the definition pattern to define terms and phrases, to give examples or illustrations of how the terms or phrases are used, and to describe how the terms and phrases apply to the course material. Each course you take has a specialized vocabulary that you will have to master and apply to do well on papers and exams. It is very important, then, that you include terms and definitions in your textbook notes. To help you recognize terms and definitions, look for the following clues:

Typographic clues. Often bold, italic, underlining, or capitalization is used to highlight a word or phrase that is going to be defined. Sometimes the term or phrase is printed in color, too. Occasionally, keywords and key phrases are repeated in the book's margins, again for emphasis.

Word clues. When authors use words like *refers to, is defined as,* and *means,* pay attention because the next phrase or clause is likely to be a definition.

Punctuation clues. Punctuation is another signal that a definition is about to be given. Look for colons, dashes, open parentheses, and commas, all of which can be used to signal that a definition follows.

Sequence Pattern

The sequence pattern is used to present a group of related items when the order of the items is critical—that is, the author's meaning will change if that order changes. The sequence pattern is used to organize chronological events, stages of development, and steps in processes. This pattern, then, is particularly relevant to textbooks on history, political science, accounting, psychology, mathematics, biology, and chemistry, all subjects that rely on sequential order for students to understand both the material and the order in which it is presented. To help you recognize the sequence pattern, look for the following clues:

Typographic clues. Sequence lists can be set off from the text with numbers and indention. When a sequence list is *narrated*—incorporated into the text—you have to read carefully to extract the items and their sequence for your notes. Often an author will use parenthetical numbers to clarify a sequence list that runs into the text; if not, watch for transitional words to help you locate both the items in the list and their sequence.

Word clues. You can identify a narrated sequence by looking for words like *first, second,* and *third,* or *and, next, following, then, later, last,* and *finally.* It is also common practice to use Arabic numbers in parentheses—(1), (2), (3), . . . —to indicate entries in a narrated sequence.

Punctuation clues. Usually a colon is used to signal the start of a sequence that is set off from the text. If the sequence is neither lengthy nor complex, a colon often is used to signal sequential order in sentences.

List Pattern

Authors use the list pattern of organization to present a group of items that are not in specific time or rank order. In other words, the order of the items in the list can be changed without changing the meaning. To help you recognize the list pattern, look for the following clues:

Typographic clues. When a list is set off from the body of the text, you often will find bullets, run-in headings, and indention used to indicate the entries in the list. Numbers should be reserved for lists where the sequence matters, but some authors use them for all the lists in a book.

Word clues. When an author chooses to narrate a list, rather than set it off, you can identify the list pattern by looking for words like *first, second,* and *third,* or *and, next, last,* and *finally.* These words may imply a numerical order, but in this context they are used for transition, not to indicate sequence. The pertinent question you should ask is whether the meaning changes if you change the order of the items in the list. If changing the order does not change the meaning, then the list pattern is being used.

Punctuation clues. Often a colon is used to alert you that a list of items follows. The sentence that introduces the list—the one that ends with the colon—may even tell you how many items are in the list.

Compare-Contrast Pattern

A *comparison* identifies the similarities between two or more items; a *contrast* points out the differences between two or more items. Many textbook authors use the compare-contrast pattern to introduce new concepts by explaining how the new concepts are similar to or different from concepts with which the students are familiar. Generally there are no typographic or punctuation clues to the compare-contrast pattern. *Like, similar, both, same, also,* and *too* are words that signal a comparison; *differ from, distinguished from, in contrast, however, unlike,* and *although* signal a contrast between two or more items.

Cause-and-Effect Pattern

Authors use the cause-and-effect pattern to describe an action, event, or circumstance (cause) and its result (effect). The sentence "If you daydream during the lecture, your notes will be incomplete" makes use of the cause-and-effect pattern. Here the cause is daydreaming and the effect is incomplete notes. Among the words that signal cause are *because, cause of,* and *reason for;* while *therefore, effect of, resulting in,* and *consequence of* signal effect. The pertinent questions to ask yourself when identifying the cause-and-effect pattern are *why* something happened and *what* were the results.

Get Connected with Writing: Using Patterns of Organization

Being able to identify patterns of organization in your textbook readings and lectures will help you organize your own thoughts when it's time to write essays and respond to short-answer exam questions. The patterns of organization used by textbook authors and lecturers are the same patterns of thinking, organizing, and presenting ideas that you can use as models when you write.

Definition Pattern

You can define terms by using synonyms, antonyms, examples, and illustrations. Use the paragraph format (see Chapter 3) and the following tips to write effective definition paragraphs. The topic sentence in a definition paragraph can be the first sentence or the final sentence of your paragraph. The transition words you use within sentences depend on whether you are using synonyms, antonyms, or classifications in your definition:

- Synonym transitions include *similar, another,* and *additionally.*
- Antonym transitions include *not, contrary, but, although,* and *even though.*
- Classification transitions include *one type, for example,* and *another kind.*

Repetition is an effective tool in definition paragraphs; it is used to emphasize the term. But don't overdo it. The conclusion of a definition paragraph is often a simple summary statement: *These three examples illustrate . . .*

Sequence Pattern

The order in a sequence paragraph is crucial to a clear understanding of the information. Sequence is the structure you would use to relate historical events, directions, and instructions, for example. Use the paragraph format (see Chapter 3) and the following tips to write effective sequence paragraphs. The topic sentence in a sequence paragraph states the topic and then the chronological events that will be presented, the number of steps involved, or the number of items to be completed: *The three stages of note taking are . . .* Transition words that can be used within and between the sentences in sequence paragraphs include *first, next, the second reason, a third item,* and *finally.*

List Pattern

The reasons, explanations, examples, or illustrations in a list paragraph are random and interchangeable. Use the paragraph format (see Chapter 3) and the following tips to write effective list paragraphs. The topic sentence in a list paragraph generally starts with the subject or topic and then states that there are a number of reasons that something occurred, or that a number of items can be included on a list. For example: *Three primary methods can be used to take good textbook notes.* Transition words that can be used within and between the sentences in list paragraphs include *first, next, the second reason, a third item, another example,* and *finally.* The concluding sentence in a list paragraph, like that of a sequence paragraph, is often a simple summary statement: *These three methods of taking notes on your textbook readings offer flexibility, accessibility, and practicality.*

Compare-Contrast Pattern

The compare-contrast pattern can be used to compare similar items, contrast different items, or both. The words you choose to introduce and discuss the items signal the nature of the pattern. Use the paragraph format (see Chapter 3) and the following tips to write effective compare-contrast paragraphs. The topic sentence in a compare-contrast paragraph identifies two or more items and states that the items are going to be compared or contrasted or both: *Two- and three-column note-taking systems share certain characteristics.* (comparison) *Two- and three-column note-taking systems are different in several ways.* (contrast) *Although two- and three-column note-taking methods share several characteristics, they are different in several ways.* (comparison-contrast)

Similarities and differences can be presented in either parallel or alternating format. *Parallel format* addresses all of the points about one item first and then, using the same structure, addresses all of the points about the second item. *Alternating format* addresses each point about both items in alternating order. Incorporate transition words into and between your body sentences to clarify the comparison or contrast you are making. For comparisons, use words like *both, and, also, too, same, similar, like,* and *each.* For contrasts, use words like *but, however, unlike, yet, whereas, in contrast, conversely,* and *while.*

Cause-and-Effect Pattern

Remember that a cause-and-effect paragraph should tell the reader *why* something happens and *what* the results of it are. Use the paragraph format (see Chapter 3) and the following tips to write effective cause-and-effect paragraphs. The topic sentence should state the subject and the focus—causes or effects—of the paragraph. This typical topic sentence would place the emphasis on the cause: *Taking good textbook notes makes studying for exams easier.* To focus on effects, rather than causes, draft a topic sentence that identifies the effects first. Here's an example: *Studying for exams is much easier with a good set of textbook and lecture notes taken throughout the semester.* Use words like *because, caused by, first cause, one factor,* and *second reason* to introduce causes; and *results from, one effect of, outcome of, consequence of, therefore,* and *thus* to introduce effects.

Have You Connected? Self-Assessment

After completing Chapter 5, answer the following questions about what you have learned.

1. Which note-taking systems are you using now to take notes on your textbook readings?

   _____

2. List at least five strategies that can help you take better lecture notes:

   1. _____

   2. _____

   3. _____

4. _____

5. _____

3. How are you using technology to help you take notes in specific courses?

_____

_____

4. List the five patterns that textbook authors and lecturers regularly use to organize materials:

1. _____

2. _____

3. _____

4. _____

5. _____

5. In the spaces below, note the five patterns of organization and at least three examples of appropriate transition words for each of them.

1. _____

2. _____

3. _____

4. _____

5. _____

Chapter 5 Summary

Taking Textbook and Lecture Notes

1. The characteristics of the many systems you can use to take notes on your readings and lectures make certain systems more appropriate for certain courses.

2. Among the most popular methods of taking notes on textbook readings are highlighting, annotating, outlining, mind mapping, and taking divided-page notes.

3. Because speed is crucial to taking good lecture notes, you should be ready to begin writing or typing as soon as the class begins; you should focus on material that is not in the textbook; you should leave space in your notes to insert information you may have missed; and you should make use of abbreviations and a personal shorthand to save time.

4. The Internet is a wonderful source of tips and examples for effective note taking.

Get Connected with Reading: Identifying Patterns of Organization

1. Your understanding of the organizational patterns used by authors and lecturers enables you to predict and make connections in your textbook and lecture materials.

2. The five most common patterns of organization are definition, sequence, list, compare-contrast, and cause-and-effect.

3. In readings, look at the typography, word choice, and punctuation for clues to organizational pattern.

Get Connected with Writing: Using Patterns of Organization

1. Using the five patterns of organization in your note taking and writing will give structure and clarity to your writing.

2. Although the strategies for writing paragraphs in each pattern of organization are very similar, you should be able to recognize the differences among them.

References

Nolting, Paul. 2002. *Winning at Math.* 4th ed. Bradenton, FL: Academic Success Press.

6 Exam-Taking Strategies

You may diligently prepare for and attend your classes and turn in all of your assignments on time, but you still may not score as high on exams as you think you should. There is help. There are strategies you can use to do better on exams. Exams are stressful. Because they are also inevitable, learning to stay calm and focused is crucial to doing well on them. You can use relaxation techniques to address the physical symptoms of stress and to help you concentrate; however, the best antidotes to exam anxiety are knowing the material and knowing how to prepare for and interpret exam questions. Although the material on your exams is going to vary from course to course, the techniques of how to approach your exams—how to relax and concentrate, how to answer objective questions, how to interpret essay prompts, how to write under pressure, and how to analyze your exam results—will stand you in good stead throughout your academic experience.

Are You Connected? Self-Assessment

Answer the following questions by circling Y for yes or N for no. Revisit this assessment after you have completed the chapter to see if any of your answers have changed.

Y   N   **1.** Do you practice good exam-taking and relaxation strategies when you prepare to take your exams?

Y   N   **2.** Do you analyze your mistakes when your exam is returned to you?

Y   N   **3.** Do you use Internet resources to help you prepare for exams?

Y   N   **4.** Do you practice answering objective questions using strategies to improve your chance of selecting the right answers?

Y   N   **5.** Do you understand directional prompts and practice writing short-answer and essay exam questions?

Learning Objectives

After completing Chapter 6, you should be able to demonstrate the following skills:

1. Understand and apply good exam-taking and relaxation strategies when you take your exams.

2. Conduct a postexam analysis to identify your mistakes and help you avoid making the same types of mistakes in the future.

3. Understand how to prepare for and apply strategies to help you answer objective exam questions.

4. Understand directional prompts and the strategies that will help you write short-answer and essay exam answers.

Study Review Plans

Ideally, you should begin reviewing at least five to seven days before your exams. If you start preparing a week before your exam, you will have time to review, reflect on the material, practice answering exam questions, and rehearse any material you have trouble with over a period of days. A sample five-day study review plan like the one described below allows you adequate time to divide the material you need to master and remember into manageable sections. This strategy should increase your comprehension and retention. The five-day plan can be compressed into three days, but you will have to work hard to cover more material each day and will have less time for review. If you find you have more than five days, the plan can easily be expanded.

Here's the five-day plan:

Day 1:   Review all of the material for your exam to get a thematic overview. Gather your textbook, textbook notes, lecture and lab notes, and any note cards you have made for vocabulary or terminology. Next, determine the number of textbook pages the exam will cover. If your professor has indicated that the exam will emphasize certain material or focus on specific types of questions, make notes about those instructions. After you complete your overview of all the material that will be on the exam, divide the material into three approximately equal parts that you will study, review, and rehearse in depth over the next three days.

Day 2:   Review and rehearse the first third of the material. Make a separate set of exam review notes that condenses your textbook notes, lecture and lab notes, and terminology note cards for this chunk of material. To condense your textbook and lecture notes and note cards, first refer to what your professor has indicated will be covered on the exam. Then, eliminate any material that will not be covered on the exam. Next, compare your textbook and lecture notes and note cards; then, when you prepare your condensed exam review notes, eliminate any duplication. Use your own words and phrases when you make your condensed exam review notes to make the material easier for you to remember. While you are making your review notes, think about the types of questions the professor is likely to ask, and then draft and answer a few sample questions.

Days 3 and 4:   Review and rehearse the second and third segments of material. Each time you review, make a separate set of exam review notes, condensing your textbook notes, lecture and lab notes, and terminology note cards. Again, while you review and rehearse, anticipate the types of questions your professor will ask, and draft and answer a few of them.

Day 5:   Review and rehearse your entire set of review notes and the mock exam questions you have written. Try to complete your studying at a reasonable hour and get a good night's sleep: You need to be alert and focused to do your best on the exam. If you are nervous about remembering the material, plan enough time so that you can review your study notes once more before the exam.

Staying Calm and Focused

Exam anxiety is a real and often traumatic experience for many students. Its effects can be physical, cognitive, and emotional. The physical manifestations of exam anxiety include nausea, difficulty breathing, shoulder and neck pain, and rapid heart rate. The cognitive effects

include difficulty remembering both before and during exams, and difficulty concentrating. The emotional effect of anxiety is negativity—a sense that no matter how hard you've studied, you are going to fail.

Relaxation Techniques

Yoga, tai chi, and meditation generally are effective methods to calm and relax the body and mind. Audiotapes of pastoral sounds, desktop fountains, and aromatherapy also reduce anxiety and improve productivity. You can achieve similar results with two easy techniques that do not require the investment of either time or money. One of these methods is based on visualization; the other is a form of relaxation exercise.

Calming visualizations. Sit in a quiet place, close your eyes, and imagine yourself in a place that is quiet and peaceful—a meadow, a forest, a deserted beach. Try to hold the scene for several minutes before opening your eyes. This technique should help you relax for at least a short time. Practice it daily for several days before an exam and on the day of the exam to help you feel more tranquil and in control during exams.

Relaxation exercises. There are dozens of relaxation exercises that will help you relieve neck and shoulder tension and loosen your grip so you don't snap your pencil into pieces. During exams you may not realize how tense you really are.

Get Connected with Relaxation Exercises

Here's a relaxation exercise for you to try. This exercise is aimed at relieving muscle tension.

1. Sit in a quiet place, close your eyes, and breathe deeply and slowly.

2. Begin with your hands. Slowly tense your hands into fists and hold for ten seconds; then relax and hold for ten seconds.

3. Next, move to your forearms, tensing and holding for ten seconds. Then, relax and hold for ten seconds.

4. Progress to your shoulders. Tense and hold for ten seconds, and then relax and hold for ten seconds.

5. Next, pull in your stomach and hold for ten seconds. Then relax and hold for ten seconds.

6. Tense your thighs and hold for ten seconds. Then relax and hold for ten seconds.

7. Point your toes up to tense and then relax your shins.

8. Raise your heels to tense and then relax your calves.

You should feel relaxed and refreshed, and ready to take an exam.

This technique may take ten to fifteen minutes at first, but you can do it in much less time with practice (Learning Center 1996).

Overcoming Negativity

Worry isn't all bad. It's that little voice inside your head that says things like, "You'd better finish that paper, or you are going to flunk this course" or "You can't go out tonight because you didn't finish studying for your exam tomorrow morning." But too much negativity can convince you that you are going to fail no matter what, so you may as well just give up. Or it can leave you unable to focus on preparing for an exam or taking it, so you leave questions blank or just quit early.

To overcome disabling negativity, you need to replace your doom-and-gloom thinking with positive thinking. One way to do that is through positive self-talk. Here are some examples of negative self-talk turned positive:

- Don't say, "No matter how hard I study, I will fail." Instead, say, "I will study this material over the next few days and do my best."

- Don't say, "I failed the last exam, so I will fail this one too." Instead, say, "Now I know what I did wrong on the last exam and how to correct it on this one."

- Don't say, "I will go blank and not finish this exam." Instead, say, "I know a relaxation technique that is going to help me stay calm and focused on this exam."

Therapists Joseph Martorano and John Kildahl (1990) suggest that you learn to listen carefully to your inner thoughts and to isolate your negative thoughts and work on stopping your negative thoughts immediately. They contend that the longer and harder you think about failure, the more difficult it is going to be for you to replace the negative messages you keep sending yourself. By accentuating the positive in your life and reorienting yourself to envision success, you will be able to change the way you feel, which in turn will change the way you act.

Exam-Day Strategies

On exam day, be confident that you have studied and prepared for the exam and will do well. Take a deep breath, relax, and use positive self-talk to reinforce your confidence. Think of positive self-talk as sound bites that you repeat over and over to remind yourself that you have studied, know the material, understand exam-taking strategies, and are going to do well on this exam.

Once you have a copy of the exam in hand, look it over. You want to get a sense of how long it's going to take to answer the different types of questions. This preview calms you down and allows you to plan ahead so that you do not run out of time before answering all of the questions. Also use the preview to make notes in the margin of the test on items you have memorized—formulas, for example, or the acronyms and acrostics you've used to memorize information. *Acronyms* combine the first letter of each word in a series of words to form a new word that helps you remember the original words. SMARTER is an acronym that helps you remember the characteristics of well-formulated goals (see Chapter 1). *Acrostics* are silly sentences that help you remember what you have studied. Every word in an acrostic starts with a clue to an item in the series of items you are trying to remember. "Please Excuse My Dear Aunt Sally" is an acrostic to help you remember the order of operations to solve equations: parentheses, exponents, multiply, divide, add, subtract. Writing margin notes allows you to clear your mind and focus on the exam.

If you are nervous when you start the test, look for easy questions and answer them first. This will help build your self-confidence (Nolting 2002). Skip the questions you don't know, but be sure to go back later and answer them, even if you have to guess. Sometimes exams are structured so that the first few questions are the most challenging, and the easier questions are distributed in later sections of the exam. Don't panic if you don't know the answers to the first few questions. Remind yourself that exams are like games and that you are a player.

Learning from Your Mistakes

Another way to change a negative to a positive is to turn your mistakes into learning experiences. Key to this strategy is taking the time to analyze the mistakes you make on your exams. An analysis of your errors can help you develop a plan of attack for your next exam so that you don't make the same mistakes again.

The postexam analysis should be somewhat formal. It begins with a test analysis. The form in Figure 6.1 asks you to go through a test, analyze all the questions you answered incorrectly, and determine the reasons why. If you are honest when you complete your postexam analysis, you will have an excellent tool to help you do better on your next exam.

Course:	Exam:		Date:
Error Types	Questions Missed (by number)		Total
		Questions Missed	Points Lost
Careless errors			
Spelling			
Grammar			
Sentence structure			
Proofreading			
Obvious mistakes			
Direction errors			
Misread			
Misunderstood			
Ignored			
Test-taking errors			
Arrived late			
Nervousness			
Hurried			
Miscopied			
Changed answers			
Incomplete answers			
Unanswered questions			
Left early			
Concept errors			
Didn't know information			
Couldn't remember information			
Application errors			
Couldn't apply concepts			
Applied only part of concepts			
Other errors			

FIGURE **6.1**   **Exam Analysis: Which Questions Did I Miss and Why?**

Source-of-Errors Analysis

You can use the form in Figure 6.2 to help you locate and analyze the sources of your study errors. This analysis focuses on the study strategies you use to prepare for exams and on the source (textbook, lecture notes, handouts, other supplementary materials) of the information in the questions you missed. By determining the source of the problem—the area with which you are having the most difficulty—you can determine where you have to focus your efforts the next time you prepare for an exam.

Source of Errors	Total	
	Questions Missed	Points Lost
Study errors: How many of these behaviors caused me to miss questions?		
Missed classes		
Inadequate notes		
Didn't study enough		
Didn't read textbook		
Didn't mark textbook		
Didn't create study aids		
Didn't anticipate questions		
Didn't do practice exams		
Total		
Source errors: How many questions did I miss from the following sources?		
Textbook		
Lecture/lab notes		
Handouts		
Supplemental assignments		
Total		

FIGURE 6.2　Source-of-Errors Analysis

Preparation Analysis

The third part of the postexam analysis addresses problems with your study plan that might have had a negative impact on your exam grade. The questions to ask yourself are listed in Figure 6.3.

Questions	Answers
1. Approximately how much material did I study that was not on the exam?	
2. Approximately how much material did I not study that was on the exam?	
3. Did I spend enough time studying the most important material (in terms of points counted) on the exam?	
4. How many hours did I study for this course in the week before the exam?	
5. How does the amount of time I studied that week compare with the recommendation of studying 2 to 3 hours per credit hour?	
6. How many days before this exam did I review for this exam?	
7. How many hours a day did I review for this exam?	
8. How did I decide what to review for this exam?	
9. What logical conclusion about my studying habits and test taking can I draw as a result of this analysis?	
10. When can I make an appointment with my professor or a teaching assistant to discuss my a result of this exam?	
11. How do I intend to change my behaviors to improve my performance in the future?	
12. What is my target grade on my next exam?	

FIGURE 6.3　Preparation Analysis: How Prepared Was I for the Exam?

Get Connected with Technology: Exam Strategy Websites

Technology can be essential to demonstrating your knowledge and earning good grades. In some courses, you are required to take exams online. Online exams generally are accessible for a limited time and must be completed within that time. In addition, some colleges require students to log on, start, and finish each exam within a certain period. Current research supports time limits for online testing: It appears that students learn the material and actually perform better on online exams that are timed (Brothen and Wambach 2004).

To prepare for your online exams, visit your college website for tips, tutorials, and strategies. In addition, you may find these sites helpful:

- The Learning Center at the University of Texas at Austin (http://www.utexas .edu/student/utlc/lrnres/handouts.html) offers suggestions on ways to cope with stress, test anxiety (including math anxiety), and writer's block, and to prepare for answering essay and objective questions. Among other pieces of useful information on the site is a guide to surviving finals week.

- Chandler Gilbert Community College (http://www.cgc.maricopa.edu/learning/ center/online_resources.shtml) has tips on preparing for and taking exams.

- Marquette University's Educational Opportunity Program site (http://www .marquette.edu/eop/study/index.html) provides links to college sites with suggestions for studying and taking exams in math, biology, and other courses.

- The College of St. Benedict and St. John's University (http://www.csbsju.edu/ academicadvising/helplist.htm) offer test-taking strategies, essay exam strategies, and stress management information.

- York University in Toronto maintains a website (http://www.yorku/ca/cdc/lsp/ index.htm) with PowerPoint presentations on stress, exams, and preparing for online tests.

There are many other Internet sources that offer exam-taking strategies, relaxation techniques, and postexam analyses that can help you do better on exams.

Get Connected with Reading: Objective Exam Questions

Developing a study review plan and remembering exam-taking strategies, learning to relax, using positive self-talk, and analyzing your mistakes—all of these techniques can help you improve your performance on exams. Exams contain different types of questions that you can learn to master. *Objective questions,* which ask you to choose one (or more) "best answers" from two or more possible answers, are common exam questions. As a general rule, objective questions are based on facts or details that are undisputed.

The most common types of objective questions are true/false, multiple-choice, matching, and fill-in-the-blank. These questions usually are structured so that there is only one correct answer. Understanding how objective questions are structured and learning strategies to approach them can help you score better on your exams.

True/False Questions

The key to answering a true/false question is determining if any part of the statement is false. If any part of the statement is false, then the entire statement is false. Conversely, to be true, a statement must be 100 percent true. Here are a number of strategies for approaching true/false questions on an exam:

1. Read the entire statement carefully. A single word can be the difference between a true statement and a false statement.

2. To avoid confusion, divide long statements into clauses. Decide if each of the clauses is true or not. Remember, if one part of a statement is false, then the entire statement is false.

3. Look carefully for absolute words, like *all, always, only, never, totally, absolutely, none,* and *entirely.* These words provide for no exceptions and virtually always make the statement false.

4. Look carefully for qualifying words, like *some, most, generally, usually, often, frequently,* and *may.* These words allow for exceptions and may make a statement true that otherwise would be false.

5. Don't be misled by thinking that a statement is true if it contains a reason. Often reasons are given for false statements.

6. Think carefully about long statements. Longer statements tend to be true because your professor wants you to remember correct information.

7. Eliminate double negatives in a statement and then reread the statement before deciding whether it is true or false. Professors often insert double negatives simply to confuse you.

8. Answer all of the questions even if you have to guess. On true/false questions, you have a 50 percent chance of guessing correctly.

Multiple-Choice Questions

The most common type of objective exam question by far is multiple-choice. Ideally, you will be able to remember the material you studied and recognize the correct choice even if the wording has been changed or paraphrased. This is Plan A. However, Plan A does not always work the way you intend, in which case you will have to move on to Plan B.

Plan A strategies. Use these strategies first when answering multiple-choice exam questions:

1. Read the *stem,* the main part of the question, without looking at the answers. Read carefully, watching especially for qualifying words such as *except, but,* and *not.* These words signal that you are looking for an exception, the only wrong answer among a number of correct answers.

2. Think about what the answer should be before you look at the choices. This strategy helps you visualize the answer and can keep you from becoming confused when all of the choices seem to be based on familiar information.

3. Read all of the choices even if you think the right answer is "a" (the first choice). Another choice may be better than "a" because it is more specific or detailed. Also, some multiple-choice answers combine two or more answers—for example, "both a and b" or "all of the above." These combined-choice answers also may be better than your original choice.

4. Remember to look carefully at the "all of the above" choice when you are sure that two of the choices are correct and selecting only two answers—"both a and b"—is not an option. Even if you are not certain that the third choice is correct, when two of the choices are correct, the third will also be correct. For example: Of the following, which can help you stay focused during an exam?

   a. calming visualizations

   b. relaxation exercises

   c. yoga, tai chi, and meditation

   d. all of the above

   After you read the stem of this question and think about the answer, you are certain that choices "b" and "c" are correct, but you cannot remember reading anything about choice "a." Because you do not have an option to choose "both b and c," you should assume that "a" is also correct. Therefore, the answer you should select is "d. all of the above."

5. Select "none of the above" as your answer only when you are sure that all of the other choices are flawed.

Plan B strategies. If you have tried the Plan A strategies and have not been able to choose an answer, then try the following strategies:

1. Read the stem followed by choice "a," and ask yourself if the statement is true or false. If it's not true, continue reading the stem with each of the remaining choices in turn, repeating the true/false question.

2. Watch for absolute words (*all, always, only, never, totally, absolutely, none, entirely*) in the answer choices. Remember that they almost always make an answer false.

3. Watch for qualifying words (*some, most, generally, usually, often, frequently, may*) in the answer choices. Remember that they often make an answer true.

4. Eliminate choices that seem irrelevant, wrong, or foolish.

5. Eliminate as many incorrect choices as possible to increase your chance of getting the right answer.

6. Avoid choices that contain words or terms that you do not know until you have exhausted all other possibilities.

7. Remember that the longest answer may be the correct one.

8. Averages sometimes work in number and date questions. To use this strategy, eliminate the high and the low numbers, and look at the remaining choices.

Changing your multiple-choice answers. You may have some preconceived notions about whether or not you should change your answers when you review objective questions on your exams. You may have heard that your first instinct is usually right, that you should stick with it and not change your answer. Researchers have found that college professors, like many students, believe that changing answers is not a good idea. When asked if changing answers helps or hinders students' test scores, more than 50 percent of the professors surveyed responded that changing answers lowers test scores. Only about 15 percent believed that changing answers would improve students' exam scores. Currently, no studies conclusively prove—or disprove—the theory that first choices tend to be most accurate (Skinner 1983, vos Savant 2004).

On the other hand, logic suggests that by the time you finish an exam, you may remember information that did not come to mind when you answered some of the multiple-choice questions. Using this theory, you might score better if you were to read the questions again and change those answers that no longer seem right. Although there is no scientific evidence that your first answer is the best answer, there is research on changing answers. For example, Skinner (1983) reports several findings that may surprise you:

- Approximately 50 percent of changed answers are changed from wrong to right.

- Approximately 25 percent of changed answers are changed from right to wrong.

- Approximately 25 percent of changed answers are changed from wrong to wrong.

Although the research that has been conducted on multiple-choice exams cannot solve your dilemma when you are in an exam trying to decide whether to change your answer to a specific multiple-choice question, knowing your odds may give you the confidence to go ahead.

Matching Questions

Matching questions are set up in two columns, generally with numbered terms or phrases in one column and lettered definitions, explanations, or examples in the second. Your task is to match each numbered item with its best description or definition in the lettered column. Try the following strategies for matching questions:

1. Look at how the columns are organized.

2. Read through the column with the shorter statements first.

3. Then, to minimize confusion, start working from the column with the longer statements.

4. Match the answers that you are certain of first.

5. Cross off choices that you have used as you go. This allows you to see what's left and to make educated guesses if necessary.

6. Use a process of elimination to find as many other matches as you can.

7. Guess at the remaining answers, using your judgment to make your best guesses.

8. Use each matching letter or number only once unless the directions tell you that you can repeat letters or numbers.

Fill-in-the-Blank Questions

Fill-in-the-blank, or sentence-completion, questions require you to supply a missing word or phrase. The following strategies can help you make good choices:

1. Read the sentence carefully, paying attention to the syntax, or word order. Determine which part of speech would fit into the blank. Even if you cannot recall the exact information, knowing whether the missing word should be a noun, a verb, an adverb, or an adjective can help you make an educated guess.

2. Look for grammatical clues to characteristics of the missing word. A blank preceded by the article *a* tells you that the next word begins with a consonant. A blank preceded by the article *an* indicates that the next word begins with a vowel. Other grammatical clues can signal the verb tense, number, or gender of the missing word or words.

3. Look at the number of blanks to get an idea of how many words you need to supply.

4. Look at the length of the blanks. Some professors vary the length of the blanks to match the length of the missing words.

5. Read blanks that appear in different clauses as separate sentences to get ideas about the logic of the missing words.

6. Remember that the words you supply must be factually and grammatically correct and must make sense in the context.

7. If you do not know the exact words wanted, guess.

Get Connected with Writing: Subjective Exam Questions

Reading skills are key to answering objective exam questions; writing skills come into play when an exam asks *subjective questions,* questions that generally require you to write a short answer, usually a single paragraph, or an essay of five or more paragraphs. What distinguishes this writing from other writing you do for your courses is the pressure of the exam situation. To perform well on subjective questions, you must come to the exam prepared, you must understand what the question is asking you to do, and you must have strategies in hand for writing under pressure.

Preparing for Essay Exams

You can prepare for short-answer and essay exams with this five-step procedure:

Step 1. Prepare. Learn as much as you can about the format of the exam. Your professors may also tell you whether or not you will have any choices to make: That is, whether you may be able to choose two of three possible essay questions. The point value of questions is also important. Suppose an exam consists of four short-answer questions worth 10 points each and two essay questions worth 30 points each. With this information, you can anticipate what to study and how to divide your time during the exam to score the most points.

Step 2. Organize. Once you have an idea of the material that will be on the written exam and the types of questions, gather all of your textbook, lecture, and lab notes, handouts, supplemental readings, and vocabulary note cards or lists. Use those materials to create condensed study review notes on the topics that will be on the exam. Your study review notes should contain lists or outlines of comparisons and contrasts, causes and effects, and processes applicable to the material.

Step 3. Review. Work alone or with a study group to review and rehearse the material, develop acronyms or acrostics to help you remember the material, and make a list of the applicable vocabulary to study for meaning and spelling.

Step 4. Practice. Think about the material and develop several short-answer or essay questions based on it. Write your answers, timing yourself on each one. Being aware of time constraints when you practice can make you more efficient during the actual exam.

Step 5. Evaluate. Check your practice short-answer and essay question answers carefully for unity, coherence, thesis statements, topic sentences, the quality of supporting details and examples, spelling, punctuation, and grammatical errors. Then look at the corrections that you have to make and try another practice question.

Understanding Directional Prompts

One key to doing well on short-answer and essay questions is understanding the directional prompts for each question. The prompts tell you what to do and what is expected in your written answers. If you do not follow the directions, you may lose a significant number of points on your answers. Table 6.1 lists a number of directional prompts commonly used in short-answer and essay questions. Before you start writing the answer to a short-answer or essay question, write down the directional prompt and make preliminary notes about what you want to include in your answer. Writing the directional prompts down on paper will help you focus and stay on point when you are planning and writing your answers.

TABLE **6.1**   **Directional Prompts**

analyze:	separate into sections, and discuss each section
compare:	identify and discuss similarities
contrast:	identify and discuss differences
criticize:	explain positive and negative points, and decide which is more prevalent
define:	provide meaning and examples
describe:	explain with details
discuss:	explain all positions and opinions
evaluate:	identify positives and negatives, and make a judgment
illustrate:	provide examples of the most important characteristics
interpret:	explain meaning with clear, concise details
justify:	provide facts, evidence, or reasons for your position
list:	provide a series of examples or points
prove:	support your position with facts
relate:	show the connections (including causes and effects) among ideas or items
summarize:	write a condensed version of the main points and major details

Writing Under Pressure

Your first inclination when you get your short-answer or essay exam questions is to start writing. After all, the clock is ticking. But instead of succumbing to the impulse to start writing immediately, take a deep breath and try following these strategies:

1. Preview the exam. Look at the number of questions that have to be answered and the approximate length the answers should be. Essay answers will be longer and require more time and effort than short-answer questions.

2. Develop a time plan that will allow you to answer all of the questions and leave you time to review and proofread your answers and make necessary corrections.

3. Figure out the order in which you should answer the questions. Consider the point value of each question in making your decision. You want to score as many points as possible, so you may want to start with a question that is worth 25 points rather than one that is worth only 5 points.

4. Read the first question you have decided to answer, and then stop and think about what you know about the topic and what the directional prompt indicates you should do with the topic. Also pay attention to the directions on how long your written answer should be.

5. Organize your thoughts on your short-answer paragraph or your essay. You can freewrite, make an outline, write a list, draw a mind map, or create a T-bar (Figure 6.4) that shows the connections among directional prompt, topic, topic sentence or thesis statement, and the major details or examples you plan to use. A T-bar works well when your directional prompts ask you to choose a side or a position.

6. You can use the margins on the exam, the cover of your blue book, or scratch paper to make your outline, list, mind map, or T-bar. Remember to address the directional prompts in your topic sentence (short answer) or thesis statement (essay).

7. Write your short answer or essay, referring to your freewriting, outline, list, mind map, or T-bar as you write. Work quickly, neatly, and efficiently because you only have time for a single draft. Concentrate on incorporating applicable vocabulary and on using correct punctuation, grammar, and spelling to save the time necessary for corrections during your final proofreading.

8. If you are not working at a computer, write or print legibly so that your exam is easy to read.

9. Leave enough space within and at the end of your answers to add any afterthoughts about the question.

For	Against

FIGURE **6.4**   **Sample T-Bar**

10. Answer all of the required questions in the time you allotted for each question and in the order you decided on.

11. Reserve the last five to ten minutes to proofread and make any necessary corrections, additions, or deletions.

Have You Connected? Self-Assessment

After you have completed Chapter 6, answer the following questions about what you have learned:

1. What exam-taking strategies will you use to prepare for and take your next exam?

   _____

   _____

2. What type of analysis are you going to use after your next exam?

   _____

3. What Internet resources have you found to help you prepare for your exams?

   _____

   _____

4. Which strategies will you use to help you answer objective exam questions?

   True/false questions: _____

   _____

   Multiple-choice questions: _____

   _____

   Matching questions: _____

   _____

   Fill-in-the-blank questions: _____

   _____

5. How will you prepare to write short-answer and essay exam questions?

   _____

   _____

Chapter 6 Summary

Exam-Taking Strategies

1. A five-day study review plan that organizes and distributes your exam preparation over several days can help you master and retain the information you need to know to do well on an exam.

2. Stay calm and focused during your exams by using relaxation exercises and positive self-talk.

3. On the day of the exam, previewing the test will give you time to calm down and develop your plan of attack. Noting formulas, lists, and terms you have memorized in the margins of the exam will allow you to focus on the exam instead of on the material you've memorized.

4. To learn from your mistakes, your postexam analysis should include an examination of the types of errors you made and the points you lost because of them, the sources of your errors and the areas where your preparation fell short, and the design of new strategies to help you avoid making the same mistakes again.

5. Use the Internet for tutorials, articles, and other sources of information about exam strategies and stress reduction, and for practice questions.

Get Connected with Reading: Objective Exam Questions

1. Objective questions generally have one correct answer.

2. Use strategies to answer true/false, multiple-choice, matching, and fill-in-the-blank questions.

Get Connected with Writing: Subjective Exam Questions

1. To prepare for short-answer and essay exams, follow a five-step process: (1) predict what will be on the exam, (2) organize what to study, (3) review what you need to remember, (4) practice writing timed paragraphs and essays, and (5) evaluate what you've written and try again.

2. Look for directional prompts to help you structure your answers on written exams.

3. To write under pressure on a short-answer or essay exam, (1) preview the exam; (2) develop a time plan; (3) determine the order in which you should answer the questions; (4) read each question, paying close attention to directional prompts and directions; (5) organize your thoughts by freewriting, listing, outlining, or creating a T-bar; (6) use the margins of the exam for notes on your answers; (7) working quickly, write your short answer or essay; (8) write or print legibly; (9) leave space for afterthoughts; (10) stay within the time limits you set and work in the order you determined; and (11) save five to ten minutes to proofread and correct your work.

References

Brothen, Thomas, and Catherine Wambach. 2004. "The Value of Time Limits on Internet Quizzes." *Teaching of Psychology* 31, no. 1 (Winter): 62–65.

Learning Center, University of Texas at Austin. 1996. "Relaxation Procedures." No. 1452.

Martorano, Joseph, and John P. Kildahl. 1990. "Climb Out of Depression." *Prevention* 42, no. 10 (October): 46–59.

Nolting, Paul D. 2002. *Winning at Math*. 4th ed. Bradenton, FL: Academic Success Press.

Skinner, Nicholas F. 1983. "Switching Answers on Multiple-Choice Questions: Shrewdness or Shibboleth?" *Teaching of Psychology* 10, no. 4 (December): 220–223.

vos Savant, Marilyn. 2004. "Ask Marilyn." *Parade,* February 29, 6.

7 Communicating Effectively

Communicating effectively involves a number of skills: making oral presentations, listening to lectures, participating in group discussions, using body language when you are speaking and listening to convey your feelings, and using proper etiquette when communicating electronically. To be successful in college and in your professional and personal life, you must be able to communicate your thoughts and ideas clearly and effectively. In your college courses, you will be required to make and listen to oral presentations, collaborate effectively with other students, and express yourself articulately via e-mail and voice mail.

In this chapter, you will focus on communications: speaking, listening, using body language, participating in group discussions, and using technology to communicate. You will also learn about identifying point of view in readings and using your point of view to write effective persuasive essays.

Are You Connected? Self-Assessment

Answer the following questions by circling Y for yes or N for no. Revisit this assessment after you have completed the chapter to see if any of your answers have changed.

Y   N   **1.** Do you know how to prepare for and practice before you make oral presentations?

Y   N   **2.** Do you know strategies to use to make you a better speaker, listener, and discussion group member?

Y   N   **3.** Do you practice good etiquette when you communicate electronically?

Y   N   **4.** Can you explain what *point of view* means?

Y   N   **5.** Do you know how to use point of view to write effective persuasive essays?

Learning Objectives

After completing Chapter 7, you should be able to demonstrate the following skills:

1. Understand and apply the principles of effective oral presentations.

2. Be familiar with strategies you can use to listen and communicate effectively.

3. Understand and identify point of view in your reading assignments.

4. Know the techniques involved in writing effective persuasive essays.

Speaking Effectively

As you sit in a lecture, you probably do not think about the preparations your professor made before class or whether your professor is comfortable addressing a lecture hall full of students. What if you, instead of your professor, had to make the presentation? How would you prepare? How would you feel if it were you standing behind the lectern facing your classmates? Making a speech may be one of the most difficult tasks you are called upon to perform during your college experience.

The thought of standing up in front of a group and speaking may make you cringe (Seligson 2005). Stage fright affects people from all walks of life: Professional athletes, movie stars, even politicians can be nervous when they have to speak before a live audience. For example, television, film, and recording star Jennifer Love Hewitt is among the celebrities who have disclosed a fear of public speaking (Brady 2005). Although speaking before a live audience can intimidate even the most polished orator, there is help for you. Preparation and practice before you take the spotlight can help you deliver an engaging presentation that will focus your audience on your message, not you personally.

Preparing for Oral Presentations

There are four basic elements in an oral presentation. Figure 7.1 is an outline showing the basic elements of an oral presentation.

> I. Attention-getter
>
> II. Introduction
>   A. Topic or thesis
>   B. Credibility
>   C. Significance of the topic
>   D. Outline of the main points
>
> III. Body of the presentation
>   A. Details and examples
>   of the main points
>   B. Visual aids
>
> IV. Conclusion

FIGURE **7.1**   **Basic Elements of an Oral Presentation**

The *attention-getter* is just that—something to grab the audience's attention. Start your presentation with an anecdote, a joke, even a startling statement. You want your listeners to focus on what you're saying.

The *introduction* combines four functions. Here is where you state your topic or thesis, the main idea of your speech or the most important point you intend to make. Next you want to establish your credibility, what it is that makes you competent to talk on this topic. You might cite personal knowledge or experience, or research you've done on the topic. Then you should explain why the topic is significant, important, or interesting. Finally, give an overview of the speech, an outline of your main points.

The *body of the presentation* is where you set out the details and examples that support your thesis. Where there is a sequence to the points, follow that sequence: Present the points in chronological or rank order. Whatever the order, be sure to use transitions to connect your points and to help your audience follow your thinking. Use visual aids in the body of the presentation to clarify your points.

You should finish with a *conclusion* that can be a summary, a persuasive argument, or a rhetorical question that will leave your audience with something to think about.

If Figure 7.1 seems familiar, then you are making the connection between the organizational principles for oral presentations and essays (see Chapter 3). Both essays and oral presentations require an introduction and thesis statement, the orderly arrangement of points and examples, and a conclusion. True, the language is different—spoken language tends to be less formal—and the final order is somewhat different. But once you have your presentation completed in essay form, you can simply rearrange it for oral delivery.

Get Connected with Writing Your Oral Presentation

In this practice, you will write an essay of no more than five paragraphs to serve as the basis for an oral presentation.

Step 1. Choose a Topic

The subject needs to be narrow because of the five-paragraph limitation. Begin by selecting an area. What area do you know about? What interests you? What do you think will interest your classmates? Do you think there is more information available to you in a particular area? Write the area you want to discuss in the space below.

Subject area: _____

Step 2. Gather and Organize Your Ideas

Head to the campus library or search online for information you can use in your presentation. Then, in the space below, freewrite, list, or outline everything you know about the topic you selected. Review your freewriting, list, or outline, and put a check mark next to the three points you want to make in your speech. Be sure that they are related in some way.

_____

_____

_____

Step 3. Decide How You Want to Present Your Topic

Choose the tone (see Chapter 4) you want to use for your speech, and write it in the space below.

Tone: _____

Step 4. Think About Visual Aids

Look back at the three ideas or examples you marked in step 2. Now, think about a visual aid you could use to illustrate one of the ideas you have selected. This is a short speech, so plan on using just one visual aid. Describe it in the space below.

Visual aid: _____

Step 5. Draft Your Attention-Getter

Think about something you can say that will grab your listeners' attention. Write it in the space below.

Attention-getter: _____

Step 6. Draft Your Thesis Statement and Introduction

Start with your thesis statement and then include information to support your credibility and the significance of your topic. Finish with a brief overview of your speech.

Thesis statement: _____

Credibility: _____

Significance: _____

Overview: _____

Step 7. Draft and Review the Body of Your Speech

Write the body of your speech in essay format, devoting a short paragraph to each of the concepts or examples you selected. Be sure your topic sentences connect the concepts to the topic of your speech.

Body paragraph 1: _____

_____

_____

Body paragraph 2: _____

_____

_____

Body paragraph 3: _____

_____

_____

Review the draft, paying close attention to the organization. Is the material easy to follow? Have you used transition words, signal words, and other clues to help your listeners make the connections between and among your ideas?

Step 8. Write Your Conclusion

Think about the tone of your speech and your audience, and choose a conclusion to use in your presentation. Practice writing conclusions by drafting three different concluding sentences in the spaces below.

Summary: _____

_____

Question: _____

_____

Persuasive argument: _____

_____

By writing your oral presentation as an essay, you can ensure that it is well organized and logical. Also, the essay becomes the basis for the outline or note cards you will use to rehearse your presentation.

Practicing for Oral Presentations

After you finish writing your presentation, review what you've written and note the most important points on index cards. Be brief. Don't use sentences; just use words and phrases that will help you remember the points you want to make. When you make note cards, write down only the beginning phrase for each point you want to make and write only on one side of the cards. When you're practicing, you don't want to pause or fumble with the cards trying to see what's on the other side. You want to deliver the speech smoothly and flawlessly, and that's what you want to practice doing. On the note card below, write in the title of your practice speech and three cues to help you remember the order and organization of the speech.

```
Title:


Cue 1:

Cue 2:

Cue 3:
```

FIGURE **7.2**   **Oral Presentation Note Card**

Writing note cards is important on two counts: to clarify the key points in your speech and to help you memorize your speech. Practice until you can make your presentation without using the note cards. Remember that your assignment is to give an oral presentation, not an oral reading. By the same token, you need to do more than recite word for word what you've written. As you practice, focus on the main points of your written presentation and the organization there. That's what the cues on your note cards are for. But the words you learn, the speech you memorize, should reflect adaptations you've made to the oral form of the delivery. It's that adapted presentation you want to know so well that the words flow effortlessly when you begin to talk.

Practice by Simulation

Practice alone, in front of a mirror, with a tape recorder or with a camcorder, until you know your presentation by heart. The key here is seeing and hearing yourself as you give your presentation. You want to know how you look and sound so that you can make adjustments to your posture, tone, and delivery if necessary. You can also use a tape recorder or camcorder to time your presentation, again so that you can make adjustments, adding or deleting material so that the length of the presentation falls within the guidelines of your assignment.

After you have practiced alone and are confident that you know your speech, try giving your speech to a live audience. Study groups are excellent forums for rehearsing oral presentations. If it is not possible to practice with a study group, recruit one or two friends, family members, or class members to be your trial audience. Work on making eye contact with the members of your audience instead of looking over their heads, at your shoes, or at the ceiling. When you're done, ask your trial audience to critique your presentation; then work on correcting any concerns audience members raise.

As much as possible, rehearse your speech in a setting that closely resembles the room where you will give your speech. If that room has a lectern, blackboard, or projector that you will use, ideally you should practice in a room with a lectern, blackboard, or projector. It is also very important to use your visual aids when you practice. Whether you decide to show slides or do a demonstration, you will feel more comfortable when you make your presentation if you incorporate your visual aids into your practice.

Practice Being a Performer

The difference between turning in a written assignment and making an oral presentation is you. Your tone, your delivery, your body language, your clothing—all contribute to the effectiveness of what you are saying. Both the tone of your voice and the tone of your presentation can help you connect with your audience. Your delivery—which includes your timing and the emphasis you place on the most important points in your presentation—is critical. Remember to speak clearly and slowly, and to emphasize what's important, so that your listeners can follow and appreciate what you're saying.

What you don't want to do is bore your audience. Think back to the most boring speech you ever heard. Was the problem with the material or the speaker? It may well have been that the speaker mumbled or talked in a monotone. Or perhaps he or she stood frozen behind the lectern, never moving, never reacting. Use your experience as a listener to be a better speaker: Don't make the delivery mistakes you have been subjected to as a member of the audience.

If you have enough space in the setting where you will be giving your speech, change positions now and again, or even move around. Movement is energy that your audience can feel; it also can help alleviate your initial nervousness. Of course, there is a line here between controlled movements and frantic movements. You don't want to pace as you speak or move around so much that you distract your audience from the message you are delivering.

Even if you do not choose to move around during your speech, you may have to change positions to demonstrate your visual aids. Practice changing positions as you rehearse your speech so that you will be relaxed and comfortable doing so. If you are required to spend most of your presentation time behind a lectern, practice with one so you are not gripping the sides of the lectern for dear life, leaning, slouching, or standing in a rigid tin-soldier pose.

Dress comfortably but appropriately when you give your speech. With so many other things to think about on the day of your presentation, the last thing you need to worry about is the appearance of your clothes, shoes, or hair.

You've written; you've practiced. You're on. When you take your place in front of the class, take a deep breath, and remember that you are prepared. Use positive self-talk (see Chapter 6) to boost your self-confidence: Remind yourself that your professor and your classmates want you to succeed and that they want to hear what you have to say (Seligson 2005). Envision yourself giving an engaging speech. Then smile and be yourself. You have your own unique style; be proud of it and of yourself.

Using Effective Body Language

As you rehearse for your oral presentation and smile, frown, gesture, or change positions you are using nonverbal communication, also referred to as *body language.* Body language is a broad generic term that encompasses using body movements, positions, and nonverbal means of communication to express feelings and emotions. Your body language as a speaker sends messages to your audience. For example, if you exhibit a brisk pace and erect stance when you approach the lectern to make your oral presentation, you transmit the message that you are confident. On the other hand if you approach the lectern with your hands in your pockets and shoulders hunched, you telegraph a feeling of dejection to your audience. If you gesture during your speech with open palms, you signal sincerity, but if you stand with your hands on your hips or behind your back, you transmit feelings of aggression, anger, and apprehension to your audience (SPARC 2006).

Making oral presentations will help you appreciate just how much the attitudes, body language, and attentiveness of the audience affect the speaker and how your body language affects others. Often students do not realize how disconcerting their actions and activities are to the professor, student, or supervisor making a presentation. During your oral presentation, how would you feel if members of your audience were engaged in these activities?

- looking out the window
- scowling or smirking
- looking at the clock above your head and not you
- playing games or text messaging
- sleeping
- tapping their fingers

These activities do not make noise that would compete with your oral presentation or your professor's lecture; however, each of these activities relays a clear message about the perceived value of what is being said. Do you realize that when you sit with your arms crossed you signal defensiveness? Or if you cross your legs and kick your foot slightly, your body language conveys that you are bored. If you drum your fingers, you show impatience, and playing with your hair signals insecurity. Rubbing your nose or pinching the bridge of your nose shows rejection or a negative evaluation (SPARC 2006).

Get Connected with Your Body Language

Answer the following questions by circling Y for yes or N for no.

Y   N   **1.** Do you look directly at the person speaking until he or she has finished talking?

Y   N   **2.** Do you maintain good posture and tilt your head or lean slightly toward the person speaking?

Y   N   **3.** Do you sit in a relaxed position without crossing your legs when you are listening?

Y   N   **4.** Do you smile or nod when you listen?

Y   N   **5.** Do you rub your hands or rest your hand on your cheek while you are listening?

Each of the nonverbal behaviors above sends a positive signal to the speaker. Give yourself 20 points for each Y for yes answer you marked. Practice limiting the negative behaviors or N for no answers you marked during the next lecture you attend.

Listening Effectively

Listening is a skill that affects every aspect of your life: academic, professional, personal. Listening behaviors influence how much you really get out of lectures or study group meetings and will affect how well you perform on your exams. If you tune out or daydream during lectures, then you will not have the information you need in your notes to study. Your listening behaviors also affect your personal and professional life. Whether you realize it or not, your friends, family, and boss can tell whether you are really listening or just faking attention.

Researchers have found that about 85 percent of what you know is learned by listening, but that you listen attentively only about 45 percent of the time when someone else is talking. If you did not hear important lecture material, project instructions, or exam details, that information was probably given to you during the 55 percent of the time when you were not listening ("Listening Factoids" 2004).

To improve your listening skills, it is important for you to understand the dynamics of listening. Just because you are present and awake does not necessarily mean that you are listening. You may be doing a number of things other than listening during lectures. Your professor probably speaks at a rate of about 125 words per minute (Nichols 1987, 36). In the meantime, you are thinking at an average rate of 500 words per minute. It's not surprising, then, that you might become distracted, preoccupied, or bored while listening to a professor talk ("Listening Factoids" 2004). And if your professor does not move from behind the lectern or speaks slowly or in a monotone, it is even more difficult for you to focus on what he or she is saying.

It is also very difficult for you to focus on what's being said when you arrive late to and unprepared for a lecture. Most professors speak from an outline, which they lay out as they begin to speak. When you are late, you miss the lecture introduction, and may well spend the rest of the lecture trying to figure out the pattern, rationale, and sequence your professor is using.

You also will have a hard time staying focused when you know little, if anything, about the subject matter. Reading your textbook assignment or reviewing the subject of the lecture before class prepares you to understand and follow the lecture. It also simplifies note taking (see Chapter 5). If you are prepared you can focus on what your professor is saying instead of frantically scribbling notes as fast as you can or simply giving up because you are too lost and confused to catch up.

Among the listening strategies you can use to improve your listening skills in lectures are the following (Hughes 2002; Johnson 1996; Nichols 1987; Randall 2005):

- Sit in the front of the lecture hall so you can hear and see your professor. This strategy also commits you to stay for the whole lecture, because getting up to leave before the end of the lecture would be embarrassing.

- Look at your professor, not out the window or at other students. Focusing on your professor forces you to pay attention to what he or she is saying.

- Think about what your professor is saying, not about how it is being said. Don't let yourself become distracted by focusing on your professor's accent, speech pattern, pauses, or any other idiosyncrasies he or she might have.

- Avoid distractions by not sitting near students who are using computers, reading newspapers, tapping their pens, eating, or doing assignments for other classes.

- Don't tune out material that you think is boring, confusing, or difficult. Instead of faking attention or daydreaming, try to concentrate on understanding the information being presented.

- Listen in a nonjudgmental manner. Listening without bias or a preconceived attitude helps you see things as they really are, instead of how you think they should be.

- Focus on the present, not on a response or question that you might pose to your professor if the opportunity arises. Rehearsing your personal opinions and comments on the subject distracts you from your present task . . . listening.

- Take lecture notes only on material that is not in your textbook or that is new to you. Learn to concentrate on listening, not writing a verbatim transcript of the lecture.

Practice these listening strategies in social situations with your family and friends. Remember to look at the speaker and to give that person your undivided attention. Focus on paying attention without interrupting, daydreaming, or becoming distracted. Then, use these listening strategies in your lecture classes and see how much more you learn from lectures.

Another good way to practice your listening skills is to watch the news on television. Television news broadcasts simulate your lecture courses because newscasters provide both factual information and interpretation in a lecture format. While watching the news, you can practice focusing, taking notes, and thinking about the material presented.

Get Connected with Your Listening Skills

Answer the following questions by circling Y for yes or N for no. There are no right or wrong answers, only honest ones.

Y   N   **1.** Do you daydream during lectures?

Y   N   **2.** Do you fake attention when your professor or someone else is speaking?

Y   N   **3.** Do you interrupt when someone else is speaking?

Y   N   **4.** Do you tune out when your professor or someone else is speaking about a subject that is difficult or complicated?

Y   N   **5.** Do you become emotional about the subject matter and quit listening in favor of thinking about defending your opinion or attacking the speaker's position?

Give yourself 20 points for each N for no answer and 0 points for each Y for yes answer. What is your listening behavior score? If you answered Y for yes to any of the questions above, actively focus on improving the way you listen by catching yourself before you interrupt or tune out, for example.

Communicating Effectively in Study Groups

Study groups have been part of college culture and a successful learning strategy for decades. Study groups can be created for any college course, but they are most common in large lecture courses, formed by students who value small-group discussion as a learning tool. Group study allows you to share ideas, reinforce learning, prepare for exams, make new friends, and build your self-confidence.

There are three important benefits of working with study groups. First, the process can increase both your understanding and your retention of material. Typically, a study group's members divide assignments into sections, and each member is then responsible for presenting and explaining his or her section to the others. Of course, all members are expected to complete the entire assignment, not just their part of it, so that they can participate in discussions. But explaining and presenting concepts to others can enhance your own speaking skills as well as your understanding of the material. In addition, by rehearsing your presentation, you are facilitating the transfer of the material to your long-term memory. And often, when you listen to other group members explain material, you develop new insight into material that may have been confusing to you.

A second benefit of working with a study group is the experience of teamwork, an understanding of all the problem-solving and personal skills involved in working with others to accomplish a task. Working in a group demands cooperation, compromise, and focus. It also teaches self-discipline and personal responsibility: If you don't get your presentation done on time and well, you are letting down your team members in addition to yourself.

Finally, there are the social and emotional benefits of study groups, of connecting with other students. There is more to this than meeting new people. Group members function as a support system for each other, a safety net of sorts that helps them meet academic challenges. Study groups provide safe havens for you to practice your communication skills as you rehearse your oral presentations, work on improving your body language, and focus on becoming a better listener using the strategies discussed in this chapter.

The ideal study group has four to six members. Smaller groups are at a distinct disadvantage if a group member is absent, and larger groups can be difficult to manage. Although your study group can be very informal, you can increase its effectiveness by having a leader, a clerk or note taker, and a liaison to meet with your professor and ask questions. The leader, clerk, and liaison can help keep the group on task, working efficiently. You should consider rotating these roles throughout the semester, so that each group member has a turn at each role. This divides the work and the responsibility among group members.

The leader has three main responsibilities: setting meeting agendas, keeping group members on task, and monitoring discussion.

- The leader decides what chapter, project, or assignment the group will work on at each meeting.

- It's the leader's job to see to it that social or unrelated conversations don't waste valuable meeting time.

- The leader should be watching the clock, limiting discussion—or an individual's tendency to monopolize that discussion—so that all items on the agenda can be covered.

A good leader occasionally is going to step on toes. That's another reason to rotate the role of leader: Because all of the group's members know they eventually are going to have to function as the leader, they are more likely to respond with understanding and cooperation when the leader asks them to get back to the matter at hand or to move on to another section or concept.

The clerk is responsible for communications, usually via e-mail. The clerk's task is simple if the group meets at a regular time in a regular place, and if its focus is always on whatever was covered during the last class lecture. If there is a routine in place, the clerk only has to contact the group members when there's a change.

The liaison is the group's representative with the professor. The liaison is responsible for making a list of questions that group members were not able to answer during the meeting; meeting with the professor or a teaching assistant to review those questions; and reporting the responses back to the group at the next meeting.

Study groups are not without problems, however. You can avoid the risk of study group sessions turning into social hours by setting aside time after each meeting for food and talk for those who want to participate. The problem of some members contributing too much or too little to the group can be avoided by rotating leader, clerk, and liaison roles, and by requiring all group members to volunteer for and participate in discussions and making presentations to the group.

Get Connected with Technology: Making Slides and Practicing Etiquette

Making Slides for Oral Presentations

You can use your computer to create a slide presentation to accompany your oral presentation. When you are using slides in a presentation, you do not need to make notes or note cards to rehearse your speech. Instead, you will practice, learn, and give your speech referring to the copy on the slides. To make your presentation even more interesting, you can incorporate graphs, charts, clip art, photographs, sound effects, and video clips in your slide presentation. Another advantage of using slide presentations is that photographs, illustrations, and charts divert your audience's attention away from you, a strategy that can help you overcome any nervousness that may otherwise affect the delivery of your speech. Figure 7.3 is an example of what you can create using slides.

If you need help creating slides, check with your campus learning center or search for an online tutorial.

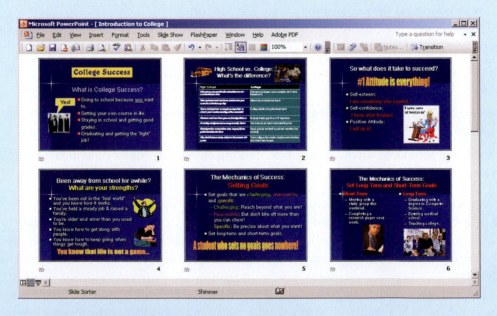

FIGURE **7.3**   **Sample PowerPoint Presentation Slides**

Cell Phone and E-mail Etiquette

Two of the most popular but often misused technologies on college campuses are cell phones and e-mail. Both are easy and convenient, but if used improperly can be disruptive, unpleasant, and reflect poorly upon you. Of course, you already know that

you should turn off your cell phone while you are in class, in the library or learning center, in study groups, or in meetings as a courtesy to other students, your professors, and the campus staff (Dave 2006). Do you realize, however, that loud and incessant talking on your cell phone in the halls or while you are in line at the bookstore or cafeteria invades the space of others who really do not want to overhear your conversations and are not impressed with your phone? Remember to exercise good judgment and practice common courtesy when you use your cell phone on campus, in the workplace, theaters, restaurants, and other public places you frequent.

E-mail etiquette (or *netiquette*) helps you make a good impression on the professor, counselor, or potential employer receiving your e-mail. When sending e-mails, you want to be concise and professional, so your e-mails should be tactful, grammatically correct, and composed as business letters. You would not write business correspondence that asked "Can U C me at 10 on Th plz?" if you wanted to make an appointment to meet with your professor during office hours. Poorly written e-mails that use text messaging shorthand or contain misspelled words and incorrect grammar do not make a very good impression. Before you send your next e-mail, take a few minutes to proofread what you have written and make the corrections necessary to convey the impression you want to make on the person receiving your e-mail.

Get Connected with Reading: Point of View

Author's Point of View

The author's point of view reflects the beliefs, theories, and opinions that influence the way the author presents information. Point of view is similar to bias. Generally, the word *bias* has a negative connotation, so if you disagree with an author's presentation of facts, you may choose to refer to the author's *bias;* but if you agree with the author, you probably would use the term *point of view* to describe how the author feels about the subject matter. Authors express a point of view on a particular subject based on their educational background, experiences, and personal feelings. An author's point of view can be identified by the positive or negative words, phrases, and language the author uses.

Reader's Point of View

As a critical reader, you should be able to identify the author's point of view, but you are not required to accept it. You have your own point of view to consider. The reader's point of view reflects the opinions that you as the reader have about the subject matter. Of course, to have a point of view you must have some knowledge about or experience with the subject, as well as your own beliefs and values. But as important as recognizing your own point of view is being able to identify opposing points of view, to better understand all of the implications of a text and to either defend your position or convince others to adopt it.

Think about point of view the next time you walk into your room. To see how many different perspectives there are, ask yourself the following questions:

What would you focus on in your room if you were a burglar?

What would you focus on in your room if you worked for a moving company?

What would you focus on in your room if you were an interior decorator?

What would you focus on in your room if you were a potential roommate?

For each of these roles, your point of view would be different. The same is true of authors. An author's point of view reflects beliefs and experience, and it reflects his or her reason for writing. If the author is simply reporting information, you are much less likely to find a bias in the writing than you would if the author is writing an opinion piece (a newspaper column, for example). Being able to identify an author's point of view, then, can also help you see other positions that the author has not included—either intentionally (to lead you to adopt his or her position) or unintentionally.

Get Connected with Writing: Persuasive Writing

Understanding point of view is important not only when reading, but also when writing. Trying to persuade someone to adopt your point of view on a subject or to change a reader's current point of view is the main purpose of persuasive writing. The ability to identify multiple positions on issues or claims will help you isolate the arguments necessary to write effective persuasive essays.

Persuasive essays argue for or against a certain course of action. The verbs used in persuasive essays that favor a course of action usually suggest that the reader *should* or *must* do something. When the writer is opposed to the action, the verbs used include *should not* or *must never*. Effective persuasive essays support the position taken with facts, examples, authoritative sources, predictions, emotional appeals, and the anticipatory rebuttal of opposing arguments.

The following strategies can help you work through the process of writing persuasive essays:

Choose a topic. One of the easiest techniques to use to get started is to frame a question that sets up at least two sides to argue: pro or con, yes or no, agree or disagree.

Gather and organize your ideas. One of the easiest ways to collect your thoughts for a persuasive essay is to make a list or use a T-bar chart (see Chapter 6). Draw a line down the middle of a sheet of paper to create your columns, and then label the columns "Yes" and "No," "For" and "Against," or "Favor" and "Oppose."

Choose a side and narrow your focus. Choose your point of view and the side you want to argue in your essay. Sometimes the choice is obvious: You can see from your list that you know more and have specific opinions about one side or the other. Once you pick a side, narrow your focus by choosing just three or four of the points you listed in step 2.

Draft your thesis statement and introduction. Draft a thesis statement and introduction that incorporate the points you want to make in your persuasive essay.

Draft your topic sentences. Outline the body paragraphs of your persuasive essay by drafting a topic sentence for each of the points you have decided to focus on. You will use these topic sentences to develop the body paragraphs of your essay. If your thesis statement establishes an order of points, use that order to arrange your body paragraphs.

Check the sequence of the body paragraphs and your transitions. Check that the order of your body paragraphs is logical and effective, and incorporate transitions that make the order of events or the order of importance clear for your reader.

Write your conclusion. Decide on the final persuasive thought you want your reader to remember and think about. In persuasive essays, the conclusion is often phrased to imply that those who do not agree with you are somehow lacking in reason or sophistication.

Proofread your essay. In addition to using the spell-check and grammar-check functions in your word-processing program, proofread your persuasive essay for errors in grammar, spelling, capitalization, sentence structure, and coherence, and make any necessary corrections.

Have You Connected? Self Assessment

After completing Chapter 7, answer the following questions about what you have learned.

1. How do you prepare for and practice before you make oral presentations?

_____

_____

2. List five strategies that will make you a better speaker, listener, and study group discussion member.

1. _____

2. _____

3. _____

4. _____

5. _____

3. What rules of cell phone and e-mail etiquette do you follow? _____

_____

_____

4. What does point of view mean? _____

_____

5. How do you use point of view to help you write effective persuasive essays?

_____

_____

Chapter 7 Summary
Communicating Effectively

1. Writing your oral presentation first as an essay will help you develop a logical and orderly speech. Practice your oral presentation alone, using a tape recorder and standing in front of a mirror, and then rehearse before a trial audience.

2. When speaking and listening, be aware of the nonverbal messages you relay through body language.

3. Good listening skills are an important factor in academic success, as well as in professional and personal relationships. Listening well requires focus, practice, and patience.

4. Study groups can provide support, academic help, and safe forums for you to practice your communication skills.

5. Technology, when used properly, can enhance your communication skills. Using slides can help add interest to an oral presentation, act as cues to help you remember, and divert the audience's attention to ease your stage fright. Cell phones and e-mails are efficient and effective communication tools when you remember to use them courteously and professionally.

Get Connected with Reading: Point of View

1. The author's point of view reflects the author's position, belief, or opinion about the subject matter.

2. You can determine an author's point of view by examining the author's word choice and language.

3. The reader's point of view refers to the position you, as the reader, take on the subject based on your knowledge, experience, or purpose.

Get Connected with Writing: Persuasive Writing

1. Persuasive essays are written to convince your reader to adopt a certain position or point of view on a subject.

2. Key to writing effective persuasive essays is choosing a side you support, choosing convincing points on which to base your argument, and leaving your readers feeling that yours is the only possible point of view on the subject.

References

Brady, James. 2005. "In Step with Jennifer Love Hewitt." *Parade,* September 18, 22.

Dave, Minauti. 2006. "Turn Off Your Cell Phone." U. Magazine. http://www.colleges.com/Umagazine/articles.taf?category=techtalk&a Summer (accessed May 31, 2006).

Hughes, Liz. 2002. "How to Be a Good Listener." *Women in Business* 54, no. 5 (September/October).

Johnson, Kenneth R. 1996. "Effective Listening Skills." Information Technology Management. http://www.itmweb.com/essay514.htm (accessed August 23, 2005).

"Listening Factoids." 2004. International Listening Association. http://www.listen.org/pages/factoids.html, September 20 (accessed August 23, 2005).

Nichols, Ralph G. 1987. "Listening Is a 10-Part Skill." *Nation's Business,* September 1, 33–36.

Randall, Vernellia. 2005. "A System for Effective Listening and Note Taking." University of Dayton. http://www.academic.udaton.edu/legaled/online/calss/note03.htm (accessed August 23, 2005).

Seligson, Tom. 2005. "They Speak for Success." *Parade,* February 20, 13.

SPARC. "Examples of Body Language." http://www.deltabravo.net/custody/body.php (accessed May 31, 2006).

Get Connected with Physical and Fiscal Fitness

As a college student, you have a great number of responsibilities in addition to attending classes, completing assignments, and studying. To maintain the endurance you need, you must eat well and exercise regularly. Your level of physical fitness—largely determined by diet and exercise—affects the amount of energy you have as well as your overall health. Equally important is exercising good judgment and making informed decisions about other health-related issues, such as alcohol consumption. You also must be able to budget and manage your money. When you are distracted or worried about something—especially money—your academic work suffers. And inadequate financial planning or indiscriminate spending can add even more stress to the pressure you are already under.

In this chapter, you will learn about strategies to help you get and stay physically and fiscally fit. In addition, you will learn how to evaluate written arguments and write expository essays.

Are You Connected? Self-Assessment

Answer the following questions by circling Y for yes or N for no. Revisit this assessment after you have completed the chapter to see if any of your answers have changed.

Y N **1.** Do you regularly eat balanced, low-fat meals that include fruit, vegetables, and whole grains, and do you exercise regularly?

Y N **2.** Do you know how to manage your finances and budget?

Y N **3.** Do you use technology to improve your physical and fiscal fitness?

Y N **4.** Do you know how to evaluate written arguments?

Y N **5.** Do you know how to write expository essays?

Learning Objectives

After completing Chapter 8, you should be able to demonstrate the following skills:

1. Understand and apply the basics of getting and staying physically fit through diet and exercise and making good lifestyle choices.

2. Understand how to manage your finances effectively.

3. Understand and apply the process used to evaluate written arguments.

4. Understand how to apply the principles of expository writing to present objective, unbiased information about a particular topic.

Getting and Staying Physically Fit

What did you have for breakfast this morning? Juice and low-sugar cereal or yogurt? Or did you have leftover pizza and a soda, or did you just skip breakfast because you were running late? The old adage, "you are what you eat," is true for everyone, but even more so for college students. You're busy, stressed, and always in a hurry, so you try to save time by going through the drive-through lane at a fast-food restaurant, eating vending machine snacks, or just skipping meals.

But do you realize that some of the foods that you turn to when you are under stress actually trigger or increase stress? Refined sugar and carbohydrates, like those found in white flour, sugar, and corn syrup, are stressors, and eating a lot of sugar in a short period of time does not give you an energy boost. Instead, it can result in hypoglycemia and cause headaches, dizziness, anxiety, and irritability. Eating the wrong kinds of fats and too many fats can prevent your body from using carbohydrates, and processed junk foods contain additives that may trigger allergies and attention deficit disorders. Too much caffeine will make you jittery and affect your ability to focus and remember (Zucker 2000).

Instead of reaching for fast foods, try substituting fish, lean meat, and egg yolks, which are high in choline, the alertness chemical in the brain. Other good brain food choices are soy products, oatmeal, rice, peanuts, and pecans, which also contain choline (Humphreys and Small 2005).

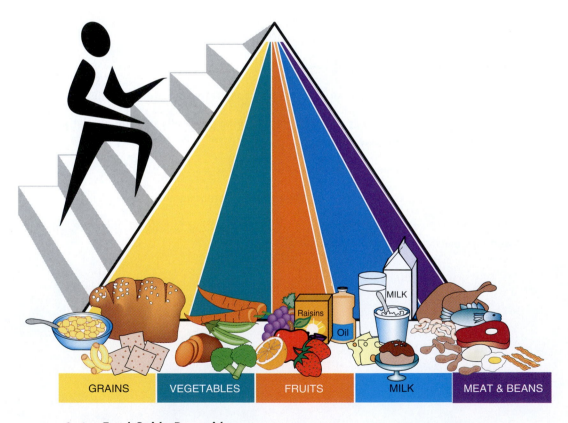

FIGURE **8.1** **Food Guide Pyramid** *Source: U.S. Department of Agriculture (http://www.MyPyramid.gov)*

The Food Guide Pyramid, Figure 8.1, will give you more information and ideas for eating a well-balanced, healthy diet, which in turn will help you feel better and perform better in your courses. If you type in your age, sex, and exercise level, My Pyramid will give you the daily recommended amounts from each of the five food groups and your daily sodium, fat, and sugar allowance.

Get Connected with Your Diet

To take control of your eating habits, try keeping a food journal for a week so you can see when and what you eat. Do you binge on sugar, salt, and fast food when you are tired? When you are nervous or worried? Or do you just turn to junk food automatically? The form in Figure 8.2 will help you create your food journal. Try to keep an accurate record of everything you eat for an entire week.

Date	Day	Time	Food	Quantity
	Monday			
	Tuesday			
	Wednesday			
	Thursday			
	Friday			
	Saturday			
	Sunday			

FIGURE **8.2** **Food Journal**

After you complete your food journal for the week, analyze your good eating habits, as well as your bad ones, and focus on determining what causes each. For example, do you eat junk food as a reward when you accomplish a difficult assignment, or do you reach for junk food to comfort yourself when you feel discouraged or lonely? If so, try to substitute a healthy food or another activity like taking a long walk to replace your junk food cravings.

It is should come as no surprise that in addition to making you tired, sluggish, and irritable, a diet of empty calories—high fat, sugar, and salt—is the leading cause of obesity. The complications associated with obesity include type 2 diabetes, hypertension, and cardiovascular disease. The Center for Disease Control and the World Health Organization have ranked obesity as one of the top health problems, now reaching epidemic proportions (Sarah W. Stedman Nutrition and Metabolism Center, 2005). As a result, federal, state, and local governments have responded by banning vending machines and fast food lunches from elementary and secondary public schools (Wallis 2004). You may dismiss these current diet-related health concerns about obesity and its consequences because obesity doesn't apply to you, at least not now. This, though, is the best time for you to develop lifelong good eating habits that will be in place when you face the stress of the workplace, family and personal crises, and the changes the future will bring your way. Despite the media, books, and advertising that promote magic pills, formulas, and miracle diets, there is no real substitute for developing nutritionally sound eating habits now.

Exercising Regularly

Within the United States, an estimated two-thirds of the adult population is overweight, and three-fifths of the nation is sedentary, so physical fitness has become a national concern (Lemonick 2004). In response, the U. S. Department of Agriculture (USDA) added exercise recommendations to its redesigned food pyramid (see Figure 8.1). The USDA guidelines recommend thirty minutes of exercise daily to lessen the risk of chronic illness, sixty minutes

a day to avoid gradual weight gain, and ninety minutes to maintain weight loss ("Dietary Guidelines for Americans" 2005).

Your schedule is already jam-packed, so how can you possibly fit in another hour for exercise? Be creative: Park farther away from classroom buildings and walk, take the stairs instead of the elevator, read your assignments while walking on a treadmill, join an intramural sports team, or take a class in dance, yoga, or weightlifting. There are dozens of ways for you to get up and get moving. You'll feel better, look better, and perform better in class. Remember that exercise also relieves stress (see Chapter 6), so try to walk, jog, or head to the gym instead of vegetating in front of the television or playing computer games with a stash of junk food snacks at hand.

Making Wise Health Choices

For most college students, drug and alcohol awareness, smoking prevention, and AIDS education were incorporated into the curriculum beginning in elementary school. Just because you are in college now and the local police department and health teachers no longer team up to present these programs to you, do not forget what you have learned.

Alcohol consumption is one of the most highly publicized as well as one of the most serious problems on college campuses. The National Institute on Alcohol Abuse and Alcoholism Task Force on College Drinking study indicates that drinking by college students contributes to 1,400 student deaths, 500,000 injuries, and 70,000 sexual assault and rape cases annually ("College Drinking" 2002). Unfortunately, despite all of the efforts to educate and warn students about potential dangers related to alcohol consumption and binge drinking, many believe that these accidents, injuries, and deaths won't happen on their campuses or to them. But they do. Jack Phoummarath was only 18 when he died of alcohol poisoning at a Texas fraternity house ("Phanta 'Jack'" 2005). An 18-year-old Miami fraternity pledge drowned while legally drunk during a hazing incident (Arthur 2004). The Duke University lacrosse team faced a national scandal stemming from the alleged rape of an exotic dancer at an off-campus party where fifteen players were charged with underage alcohol possession, open container violations, and disruptive behavior ("Duke's Lacrosse Team" 2006). Before you succumb to the temptation to do something that you really know you shouldn't do, take a few minutes to think it over and assess the risks before making your decision. To echo the phrase you've heard over and over since elementary school, remember it's okay to "Just say no!"

In addition to the health risks associated with alcohol and drugs in particular, there are legal implications for college students. Your institution's student handbook contains policies covering alcohol, drugs, smoking, and other activities that are prohibited on campus. Failure to abide by these rules may lead to your suspension or dismissal regardless of your grades or attendance record. As adults, college students also face criminal and civil liability for illicit or illegal activities (Arthur 2004). Also, many jurisdictions in the United States have adopted a zero tolerance policy for minors in possession, open containers in vehicles, driving under the influence, drunk and disorderly conduct, possession and distribution of drugs, as well as any of the unintended consequences of being impaired or intoxicated. Fermine Castillo is only 23, but he has been convicted for murder, not manslaughter or negligent homicide, because he drove under the influence of alcohol and collided head-on with a van, killing a 20-year-old passenger and injuring several others in the van (Humphrey 2006). Remember to think before you act. If what you are about to do is something you might regret, your solution is easy— don't do it even if what you plan is "just a party" or "just having fun." Making good initial judgments or alternatively discontinuing your involvement if a situation or event escalates out of control will protect you and others around you from accidents, injuries, or, in the worst-case scenarios, death and the liability for impaired judgment that will change your life forever.

Getting and Staying Fiscally Fit

Maintaining your physical fitness and making good choices about your health are important at this stage of your life, and so is being savvy about your finances. The first step toward financial solvency, which simply means having more money than debts, is understanding what you have and what you need. Money is something you can always use more of, especially when you are in school and living on a tight budget. You are already under stress trying to keep up with your course work. Not having enough money to pay your bills and expenses adds to that stress. If you have ever bounced a check or used one credit card to make payments on another, you know the feeling of losing control. More is involved than the impact of worry on the quality and timeliness of your assignments. If you have to work extra hours at your part-time job or work overtime to make payments, you may be too exhausted to study, which means you will fall behind on your assignments. If you get too far behind and cannot catch up, you may be forced to withdraw and pay for the same course again later. Withdrawing from or failing a course can limit your ability to obtain financial aid in the future. In addition, you will be obligated to repay the money you borrowed, whether you pass the course, withdraw, or fail. Clearly, budgeting and taking charge of your finances should be among your priorities.

Budget Your Way to Fiscal Fitness

Making and sticking to a budget, resisting the temptation to spend, and maintaining control of your finances will help you avoid the "spend–worry–work overtime" cycle. If you are in control of your finances, you can devote your time to studying and doing well in your courses instead of worrying about bills.

One way to take control of your finances is to inventory your financial resources and expenditures. Ideally, your resources, or income, will exceed your expenditures, so you can put away some extra money in a rainy-day account for unexpected expenses and emergencies. At the very least, you want your resources to equal your expenditures, so you break even. The worst scenario here, of course, is when your resources don't cover your expenses.

Get Connected with Your Finances

You can use the monthly budget worksheet in Figure 8.3 for your financial inventory. Begin by listing all of your monthly income and expenses, and then subtract your monthly expenses from your income to see how much over or under budget you are.

If you are over budget—if your expenses exceed your income—ask yourself how you can save or cut back on your expenses:

- Can I cancel newspaper and magazine deliveries, and read my favorite magazines and newspapers in the campus or public library?

- Is there a local textbook exchange, used-book center, or textbook rental service that can save me money on books?

- Are there textbooks that I can use in the campus library or learning center?

- Can I avoid ATM fees by using my bank's ATM machines?

- Can I eliminate or cut back on meals out, movies, and entertainment expenses?

- Can I rent or borrow movies and music or use the Internet services on campus instead of purchasing them?

- Can I plan my commuting better to save on gas or bus fares?

- Can I postpone buying new clothes, CDs, or electronic equipment?

- Can I limit my credit card and cell phone usage to avoid interest and overage fees?

- Are there hidden fees, late charges, or add-ons charged by my bank, credit card, or service providers that I can reduce or eliminate? (Brenner 2006).

If you are under budget, think about saving, not spending. Start by asking yourself what you should do with your extra money:

- Should I put some money into a money market savings account?

- Should I participate in my employer's 401(k) plan?

- Should I invest in a mutual fund?

- Should I invest in stocks or bonds?

Making and sticking to a budget will help you control your money and finances instead of having your finances control you. If you know how much you have to spend and the expenses you have to cover, you will be able to make informed and responsible decisions about what to buy and when. While you are in school, you may have to make sacrifices, defer purchases, and control your discretionary spending. These sacrifices may seem unfair or even a tremendous burden, but remember that they are only for the short term. Over the long run, the earning power of a college degree will be worth the sacrifices you make now.

Use Your Credit Wisely

Credit cards are convenient, universally accepted by merchants, and easy to acquire; but they can cause financial disaster for college students and take years to pay off (Spors 2004). Although a $20 minimum monthly payment on a credit card doesn't seem bad, few students—few adults, for that matter—realize that a $1,000 balance on a credit card with an APR of 17 percent and monthly payments of $20 will take seventeen years to pay off, assuming no other charges are made. Paying the minimum on a credit card account with a $5,000 balance translates to about forty years of payments (Spors 2004).

Instead of using credit cards, many college students resort to debit or check cards for purchases. The key to managing debit or check cards is to remember to record the date and amount of each purchase, and the amount of each check, ATM, or overdraft fee. Then at least once a month, balance or reconcile your account against your monthly statement to make sure the amount the bank says you have matches the balance recorded in your checkbook. You can usually monitor your account online or by phone in between or in lieu of waiting for monthly statements.

Category	Amount
Income:	
Wages	_____
Commissions/tips/bonuses	_____
Interest/dividends	_____
Miscellaneous income	_____
Loan proceeds	_____
Total monthly income:	_____
Expenses:	
Tuition and books	_____
Credit card/loan payments	_____
Rent/mortgage	_____
Renter's/homeowner's insurance	_____
Cable/Satellite TV	_____
Phone	_____
Car/truck payments	_____
Gasoline/fuel/oil	_____
Auto/truck repairs/maintenance/fees	_____
Auto/truck insurance	_____
Transportation fees (bus, subway, tolls)	_____
Health/dental insurance	_____
Health/dental care	_____
Computer expenses	_____
Child care	_____
Entertainment/recreation	_____
Groceries/household products	_____
Pet expenses	_____
Clothing expenses/laundry/dry cleaning	_____
Meals away from home	_____
Gifts/donations	_____
Newspapers/magazines/CD/DVD/books	_____
Miscellaneous expenses	_____
Total monthly expenses:	_____
Total monthly income − Total monthly expenses = Net monthly income	_____

Note: To convert weekly income or expenses to monthly income or expenses, multiply the weekly amount by 4.3.

FIGURE **8.3**   **Monthly Budget Worksheet**

Safeguard Your Credit and Identity

Identity theft is a very real threat that can wipe out your funds, destroy your credit, and cost you countless hours to rectify, when time is already at a premium in your busy life. Be wary of free offers and other online or telephone attempts to get you to reveal personal and financial information. Never give out your passwords, and never give out your social security number or bank or credit card account numbers unless you initiated the transaction and can verify the legitimacy and security of the site and transaction. In recent months, hackers have infiltrated and stolen thousands of social security and account numbers from allegedly secure government, bank, and university data repositories. Be sure to acknowledge and follow the instructions these institutions provide if you are notified that your personal information has been compromised.

In addition, safeguard your personal information by keeping your account passwords and cards in separate locations, so in case your wallet is ever stolen or lost a thief cannot access and clean out your accounts. Finally, be cautious regarding how and where you dispose of applications, credit solicitations, and other forms that contain your personal information. Tearing or shredding will make your trash unusable to Dumpster divers looking for the means to steal your identity.

Get Connected with Technology: Online Physical and Fiscal Fitness Tips

Physical Fitness Tips

The Internet is an excellent resource tool to help you learn more about getting physically fit. The following websites are just a few examples of what you can find to help you learn more about diet and exercise:

- Create your own food pyramid plan based on your age, gender, and activity level at MyPyramid.gov (http://mypyramid.gov/mypyramid/index.aspx), a site maintained by the U.S. Department of Agriculture.

- Play the Longevity Game at Northwestern Mutual's site (http://www.nmfn.com/tn/learnctr—lifeevents—longevity), to see predictions based on your lifestyle.

- Click on the Health Tools link on the Mayo Clinic's Healthy Living page (http://www.mayoclinic.com/findinformation/healthylivingcenter/index.cfm) for quizzes on nutrition and fitness, slide shows, and videos.

- Fitness Center (http://www.justmove.org/home.cfm), sponsored by the American Heart Association, contains exercise diaries, links to fitness resources, and fitness recommendations based on your lifestyle.

- Appalachian State University's Lose Weight site (http://webits3.appstate.edu/apples/health/Weight/default.htm) has questions and answers about diet and weight loss.

- Check college alcohol policies in the fifty states and U.S. territories at http://www.collegedrinkingprevention.gov/policies/.

- Watch and listen to the Alcohol Myths slide show at http://www.collegedrinkingprevention.gov/Collegestudents/alcoholMyths.aspx.

Fiscal Fitness Tips

There are many legitimate sites on the web that you can turn to for help living on a tight budget and spending wisely. These sites offer information on money, insurance, credit and debit cards, credit reports, identity theft protection, and credit counseling. Here are several good sites for general fiscal fitness information:

- The U.S. Department of Education has developed a site especially for college students: http://www.ed.gov/about/offices/list/oig/misused/victim.html. It's an excellent resource for information about scholarship telemarketing scams, ways to protect yourself against identity theft, and actions to take if you are a victim of identity theft. The department also has a toll-free number to call to report student-loan fraud: 1-800-MISUSED.

- Every consumer is entitled to a free annual credit report. On its site, the Federal Trade Commission (FTC) identifies the authorized online source for credit reports: https://www.annualcreditreport.com/cra/index.jsp, or you can call 877-322-8228.

- On its home page (http://ftc.gov), the FTC offers the grand scam challenge games (http://www.ftc.gov/grandscam) and has links to information for consumers, including an alert on payday loans (http://www.ftc.gov/bcp/conline/pubs/alerts/pdayalrt.htm).

- CNN's Money 101 course (http://money.cnn.com/pf/101/) can help you build your financial skills and Playbook for Life (http://www.playbook.thehartford.com) provides finance tips for college student athletes.

Get Connected with Reading: Evaluating Written Arguments

When you are asked to evaluate written arguments, such as testimonials for a new miracle diet program or exercise video, your role is much like that of a juror. Jurors are supposed to pay careful attention to the evidence admitted in court, the arguments of the attorneys for both sides, and the judge, who instructs the members of the jury on the law. The jurors are then required to begin deliberations and reach a verdict based on the judge's instructions. Try to think like a juror and use this five-step process when you evaluate your textbook reading and research assignments:

Step 1. Identify the issue. The issue is generally the main idea of the passage. Remember to ask "Who or what is this about?" to find the topic. Then ask "What is the most important point about the topic that the author makes?" (see Chapter 2).

Step 2. Identify the support. Look for the reasons, facts, opinions, data, and authorities cited on both sides of the issue. When looking for reasons, the transitions that indicate cause and effect can be helpful clues (see Chapter 5). A fact is something that can be proved objectively, making it a particularly useful criterion in evaluating an argument. Opinions cannot be proved, but they can offer valuable insight when they are based on logic, reliable and valid information, and reasonable interpretation. Data sometimes are used to support an argument, but be aware that data can be manipulated and do not necessarily tell the whole story. Remember that expert opinions or quotations from authorities are only as good as the experts providing them, so always determine whether the authorities are qualified to speak on the subject or are simply actors or paid endorsers.

Step 3. Evaluate the support. As a juror, your duty is to determine the credibility and veracity of the evidence and testimony. When you evaluate support for an argument, you perform the same analysis.

Step 4. Evaluate what is missing. Your evaluation is not complete until you analyze what should be mentioned but is not. Remember that authors present their point of view on the subject, and effective persuasive writing focuses on only one side of an issue (see Chapter 7).

Step 5. Make a decision. Use the information you have gathered while reading and analyzing the text to decide whether or not the argument is defensible, and make your decision—just as you would if you were a juror.

Throughout your college experience, your career, and in your daily life, you will be called upon to make decisions about issues on a routine basis. The more you know about using a process for making informed decisions based on the evidence, the more accurate your decisions will be.

Get Connected with Writing: Expository Writing

One of the formats that you will find most helpful when you are writing for your college courses is expository writing. This format, which explains or informs your reader about a particular subject, is familiar because it is often used in newspaper articles, encyclopedia entries, and college textbooks. The purpose and intent of expository writing is to present objective, unbiased information about a particular topic—for example, hypnosis for weight loss or smoking cessation. However, since you select the tone and the facts, bias can and often does exist in expository writing as you present the truth as you see it.

When writing expository essays, you can use the following process:

Step 1. Choose a topic. Expository essays are ideal for providing explanations of events, decisions, and policies. The key is to choose a topic that is not too broad to be addressed in an essay.

Step 2. Gather and organize your ideas. Freewrite, list, or outline your ideas and thoughts on the topic.

Step 3. Narrow your focus. Using the thoughts you've gathered in step 2, narrow the topic to three or four points that you can adequately address in an essay, making sure the points you choose are related.

Step 4. Draft your thesis statement and introduction. Your introduction and thesis statement should incorporate and be related to the main points you selected in step 3.

Step 5. Draft your topic sentences and body paragraphs. Each topic sentence should relate to one of the points you have decided to focus on in the essay. Once you have your topic sentences, draft body paragraphs that develop and explain each of the topic sentences.

Step 6. Check the sequence and transitions. Check the order of your body paragraphs to make sure the examples and points you are using to explain the topic are in the correct time sequence or order of importance. Then, incorporate transitions within and in between the body paragraphs that will help clarify the order.

Step 7. Write your conclusion. Choose the final thought that you want to leave with your reader. In expository essays, your conclusion can simply summarize the information you've presented. Remember, though, that it must be consistent with and flow naturally from your thesis statement, topic sentences, and supporting details.

Step 8. Proofread your essay. Proofread your essay for grammatical, spelling, capitalization, usage, sentence structure, and coherence errors after you use the spell-check and grammar-check programs on your computer.

Have You Connected? Self-Assessment

After completing Chapter 8, answer the following questions about what you have learned.

1. What strategies will you use to ensure that you eat a healthy, well-balanced diet and exercise every day? _____

_____

2. What strategies will you use to control your finances instead of letting them control you?

_____

_____

3. Which websites have you found useful to help you take charge of your physical and fiscal fitness? _____

_____

_____

4. List the five steps that you can use to evaluate written arguments.

    1. _____

    2. _____

    3. _____

    4. _____

    5. _____

5. What process would you use to write an expository essay? _____

_____

_____

Chapter 8 Summary

Get Connected with Physical and Fiscal Fitness

1. Eating a nutritious, well-balanced, high-protein diet, low in fat, sugar, and salt, will help you feel better, look better, and perform better in class.

2. Make informed decisions about your behavior and consider how using alcohol or drugs, or engaging in other risky behavior, will affect you physically, emotionally, and academically.

3. Making and sticking to a budget can help you gain and maintain control over your money, instead of allowing your money to control you.

4. Exercise caution to protect your personal information from identity theft.

5. Use the Internet to learn more about diet, exercise, health, and financial issues, but be cautious when conducting transactions online.

Get Connected with Reading: Evaluating Written Arguments

1. Evaluating written arguments involves a five-step process: (1) identify the issue; (2) identify the support for the argument; (3) evaluate the support; (4) determine what support is missing; (5) evaluate the argument.

2. Using this process to evaluate written arguments enables you to carry out the analysis necessary to make well-reasoned, thoughtful decisions on issues.

Get Connected with Writing: Expository Writing

1. Expository essays are informational by nature, written to explain and inform your reader about your topic.

2. To write an expository essay: (1) choose a topic; (2) gather and organize your ideas; (3) narrow your focus; (4) draft your thesis statement and introduction; (5) draft your topic sentences and body paragraphs; (6) check the sequence and transitions; (7) write your conclusion; (8) proofread your essay.

References

Arthur, Lisa. 2004. "Two Students Sued in Hazing Death." Echo online: A Reflection of the Eastern Michigan University Community. http://www.easternecho.com/cgi-bin/story.cgi?1402, February 4 (accessed June 4, 2006).

Brenner, Lynn. 2006. "Don't Let Hidden Fees Pick Your Pocket." *Parade,* June 4, 18–20.

"College Drinking Hazardous to Campus Communities." 2002. Security On Campus, Inc. News. http://www.securityoncampus.org/update/news/040902.html, April 9 (accessed June 4, 2006).

"Dietary Guidelines for Americans." 2005. United States Department of Agriculture. http://www.health.gov/dietaryguidelines/dga2995/recommendations.htm (accessed June 4, 2006).

"Duke's Lacrosse Team Suspended Pending DNA Results." March 31, 2006. ESPN.com news services http://sports.espn.go.com/ncaa/news/story?id=2387151 (accessed June 4, 2006).

Humphrey, Katie. 2006. "Prosecutors Pleased with 30-year Sentence for Murder." *Austin American Statesman,* May 21.

Humphreys, Liz, and Gary Small. 2005. "Boost My Memory." *Remedy* 12, no. 1 (Spring): 80.

"Inside the Pyramid." United States Department of Agriculture. http://www.mypyramid.gov/pyramid/ index.html (accessed August 24, 2006).

Lemonick, Michael D. 2004. "How We Grew So Big." *Time,* June 7: 59-62.

"Phanta 'Jack' Phoummarath, 18, Died of Alcohol Poisoning." 2005. I Speak of Dreams. http://www.lizditz .typepad.com/i_speak_of_dreams/2005/12/phanta_jack_pho.html (accessed June 4, 2006).

Sarah W. Stedman Nutrition and Metabolism Center, Duke University. "Clinical Research." http://www .stedman.mc.duke.edu/stedman/competencies/research.aspx (accessed July 13, 2005).

Spors, Kelly K. 2004. "Starting Out: Beware of Credit Cards at College." *Wall Street Journal,* September 5.

Wallis, Claudia. 2004. "The Obesity Warriors." *Time,* June 7: 83-84.

Zucker, Martin. 2000. "Food and Stress." *Better Nutrition.* May.

9 Get Connected with Relationships

Thus far you have learned skills and strategies that will help you reach your academic goals and be a better student. You have also learned personal physical and fiscal fitness tips that will help you be your best, so you can do your best. In this chapter, you will learn about connecting with and developing relationships with others. By learning and developing the characteristics and strategies necessary to build successful relationships in college, you will be prepared to use those same ideas to develop relationships in your community, as well as in the global economy you will become a part of in the workplace. Successful relationships are built upon ethical behavior, integrity, trust, respect, courtesy, and an appreciation of diverse cultures.

In this chapter, you will also learn about using inductive reasoning models to draw logical conclusions from your reading assignments and the organizational strategies that will help you plan and write your research papers.

Are You Connected? Self-Assessment

Answer the following questions by circling Y for yes or N for no. Revisit this assessment after you have completed the chapter to see if any of your answers have changed.

Y   N   **1.** Can you explain the meaning of the terms *ethics, integrity,* and *trust* in the context of relationships?

Y   N   **2.** Can you list three strategies that will help you build relationships with people from diverse backgrounds?

Y   N   **3.** Do you know how to use the Internet to learn about integrity, diversity, and relationships and to help you with your research papers?

Y   N   **4.** Do you know how to draw logical conclusions?

Y   N   **5.** Do you have a plan that will help you write research papers?

Learning Objectives

After completing Chapter 9, you should be able to demonstrate the following skills:

1. Understand how your behavior, integrity, and ability to communicate affect your interpersonal relationships.

2. Know how to build positive relationships with people of diverse backgrounds.

3. Understand and apply the principles of inductive reasoning to draw logical conclusions.

4. Know how to use organizational strategies to help you research and write papers.

Integrity, Ethics, and Relationships

College provides you the opportunity to reflect on your personal strengths and weakness and develop your emotional intelligence, the personal qualities apart from intellect that contribute to success. Students who learn to control their moods and impulses, focus on self-awareness, and acquire people skills become more successful than their peers who ignore the emotional side of intelligence (Goleman 1995). The best time to become the type of person you want to be is now, and the best place to begin developing the strength of character that will sustain your future relationships is during your college years.

Practice Integrity

College students are expected to exhibit a number of personal traits related to character. One of those traits is *integrity,* which involves personal honesty. Student handbooks address academic integrity often in relationship to prohibited activities: cheating, plagiarism, and unauthorized collaboration. Cheating is a broad prohibition that encompasses submitting exams, papers, projects, or quizzes that are not the product of your individual effort.

Plagiarism involves improperly using the words or ideas of others without crediting the source. To avoid plagiarism, learn and practice proper paraphrasing, which is a summary in your own words (not copying text and changing a few words), and always cite the source you use. If you have trouble properly paraphrasing the text you want to use in a paper or presentation, consider using quotations with proper punctuation and citations to avoid violating plagiarism policy.

Unauthorized collaboration occurs when you get help on an assignment without your professor's permission. From time to time, your professors will assign group projects and expect you to work collaboratively. Other assignments are intended to be only your work, not a paper or project you borrowed, bought, or persuaded someone else to prepare for you.

The academic penalties for these offenses range from failure on the assignment or in the course to suspension or expulsion. If you have not yet read your institution's student handbook or policies on academic integrity, now would be an ideal time to do so.

Integrity is also an issue in your personal life. The illegal downloading and distribution of copyrighted software, films, and music has reached alarming proportions on college campuses. Napster was the brainchild of a Boston college freshman named Shawn Fanning who wrote a file-sharing program for downloading music from the web. The resulting lawsuits bankrupted Napster and fundamentally changed the way music is distributed over the web (Dominick 2002, 207–210; Geewax 2005). Would you use pirated music, software, or movies? Have you ever bought knockoffs of designer-label clothes and accessories? Do you think it's dishonest to make copies of textbooks instead of buying them? All of these actions involve copyright infringement, a violation of federal law.

The technology you use to help you with your course work also raises many issues involving integrity. Many colleges have reacted to illegal file sharing by installing antipiracy software on their networks. For example, the University of Florida developed the Icarus program to monitor and stop downloads, and the University of Texas limits the amount of information students can download or send (Barnes 2005). Ethical questions have also been raised by the sale of college course notes, research papers, and exams on the Internet (Jesdanun 2005). Visit your college's website to learn about the ethical standards at your institution: How is illegal downloading and defined and treated at your college? What penalties does your college impose for purchasing notes, papers, projects, and exams online?

Behave Ethically

Aside from compliance with academic integrity policies that your college expects from you, you may be required to take an ethics course or a specialized course in medical, legal, or business ethics for your major. In these courses, you will study about the principles of morality and ethical theories, including patient and client confidentiality, fiduciary relationships, and legal privileges that prohibit the disclosure or use of information gained as a result of a confidential relationship. The deterioration of business and personal ethics has been in the spotlight recently as current events have focused on the illegal and illicit behavior of celebrities, business leaders, and public officials.

Sports fans and players alike have exhibited poor sportsmanship and bad judgment ("Smackdown Culture" 2004). Recently, brawls between players and fans in stadiums and arenas, human growth hormone (HGH) and steroid use, and gambling have tarnished the all-American image of professional athletes such as Pete Rose, Barry Bonds, Ron Artest, and Rafael Palmeiro (Bennett 2004; Bridges 2004; Bohls 2005; Sheridan 2004). Celebrities like Michael Jackson, Robert Blake, O.J. Simpson, and Robert Downey have faced highly publicized criminal trials (Ahrens 2005; "Feeling Vindicated" 2005). Others, like rappers Sean Combs (P. Diddy) and Beanie Sigel, for example, build their reputations on bad conduct ("Newsmakers" 2005). Martha Stewart and designer shoe-guru Steve Madden served prison sentences for perjury and securities fraud (Ahrens 2005; Berkman 2001; Seremet 2004).

Virtually all of the corporate scandals in recent years—Tyco, Enron, WorldCom, Adelphia—involved violations of ethical standards by corporate management, auditors, lawyers, financial advisors, and banks (DesJardins & McCall 2005; Chandler 2004). Government has also been rocked by the illegal and immoral behavior of public officials. House majority leader Tom DeLay and Congressmen Randy "Duke" Cunningham and William Jefferson are representative examples of the corruption, bribery, and perjury investigations that have occurred recently (Copelin 2005; "Congressman Resigns" 2005; "Affidavit: $90,000" 2006).

Build Relationships

Despite the current ethics meltdown, you expect the people you elect to public office and deal with professionally and personally to be trustworthy. In return, the people you interact with expect the same from you. Being honest, fair, and trustworthy is the first step to building relationships, networks, and connections with your professors and classmates, as well as with your family, friends, coworkers, and boyfriends or girlfriends. These are the people who can help and support you when you most need it, and they will expect the same from you when they need help. But integrity alone is not enough to build and sustain these relationships: you need people skills. Have you ever "struck out" in an interview, at a meeting, in a discussion, or on a date? What happened that caused a communication meltdown? But more importantly, what can you do to avoid the same results in the future?

Too often relationships with the people you value most break down because of communication barriers. Avoid falling into repetitious communication cycles like those that you may experience during arguments. Do differences of opinion with your family and friends deteriorate into shouting matches or leave you feeling depressed? If so, think about your speaking and listening skills and focus on the nonverbal messages you send to others (see Chapter 7). Next, consider the tone and attitude you use when communicating. When you take a superior position by criticizing, blaming, preaching, ordering, or name-calling, you put the person you are communicating with in a defensive posture, and you assume the same defensiveness when you are being attacked.

Conflict among and between people is a fact of life. The way you respond and negotiate the resolution of the situation makes the difference. There are productive and counterproductive ways to resolve the conflicts that arise in your personal and professional relationships. Always winning or always being right makes good copy for a reality television series and may soothe your ego, but won't win you many friends or help you develop meaningful relationships. Being overly aggressive intimidates others. Similarly, manipulating or duping people makes those with whom you need to build relationships feel used, abused, and resentful. A better strategy is to be assertive, which means to be factual and direct without making accusations, and to apply good problem-solving strategies (see Chapter 4).

Get Connected with Integrity, Ethics, and Relationships

Learn to negotiate effectively and find solutions that satisfy both parties: win-win situations. To do this, you have to focus on your needs and desires as well as those of others and make the best compromise you can to satisfy both sides. In other words, work on solutions that are fundamentally fair.

A simple game described in *Principles of Economics* demonstrates fairness (Mankiw 2004, 492). The game has two players. The first player proposes how to split $100 into two portions, one to keep and one to give to the other player. The other player then accepts or rejects the proposal. If the other player accepts the proposal, then the $100 is divided and distributed accordingly. However, if the other player rejects the proposal, they both walk away without anything. If you were the first player, what division of $100 would you propose? If you were the other player, what division of the $100 would you accept? You know that a split of $90 for you and $10 for the other player probably won't be accepted, and you'll end the game in a lose-lose situation. Think about this exercise the next time you have to negotiate, and focus on finding solutions that will give both parties what they need, instead of giving in to keep the peace or holding out for everything you want.

Adopt Positive Role Models

When you are working on improving your interpersonal relationship skills, do not overlook the influence of role models. A recent study conducted at Oregon State and Texas A & M Universities found that students whose role models are friends, college advisers, and clergy are less likely to use questionable ethical behavior when negotiating and resolving conflicts than students whose role models are coaches and journalists (Herring 2006).

Using positive role models and avoiding negative relationships, such as the "herd" mentality of certain groups and individuals who bring out the worst in you, will put you on the path to building positive relationships. Not only are sexual harassment, hostile environments, assault, stalking, and date rape actionable criminal offenses, they can cause an abrupt end to your academic progress if you are expelled from college. If you are in a relationship that is heading in this direction, end it before it spirals out of control, and focus on using your skills to develop more positive relationships based on trust, fairness, ethical conduct, and integrity.

Culture, Diversity, and Relationships

As you head across campus to class or sit in your classes, look around and take note of the people you see. Your college campus is a living example of diversity, bringing together people of all ages, cultures, races, and religions. On campus, you will see students, faculty, and staff from around the world. Some students in your classes may be first-year students who have just graduated from high school. Others may be older returning adult students with jobs and families to support. Some may be bilingual or bicultural. Others may have disabilities, either physical or learning related, such as attention deficit disorder (ADD) or dyslexia.

Your student handbook probably contains a section on your institution's antidiscrimination policy. Typical discrimination prohibitions include race, color, religion, national origin, age, gender, sexual orientation, political affiliation, and disabilities. Many colleges also offer assistance to students through campus offices for students with disabilities, international students, and veterans. Students who believe that they have been discriminated against typically can file complaints and have investigations initiated if, for example, they have been denied reasonable accommodations for their disabilities or have been sexually harassed.

Your student handbook is also a source for locating and joining a broad array of student organizations on campus. Typical student organizations include deaf students' clubs; Latino, African-American, and Asian groups; gay and lesbian societies; and veterans' clubs; as well as sororities, fraternities, honor societies, and student life associations. All of these student groups reflect the diversity of your college and the country itself.

The United States is a country rich in diversity, home to people of every race, ethnic origin, and belief. According to the U.S. Census Bureau (2001b), there were 281,421,906 people living in the United States in 2000, the date of the most recent census. The next census will be taken in 2010.

The pie chart in Figure 9.1 shows the 2000 census results by race.

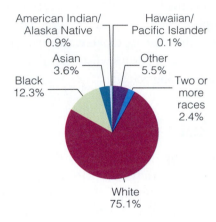

FIGURE **9.1**   **Population by Race, United States, 2000** *Source: U.S. Census Bureau (2000c).*

Notes: Missing from the chart is a category for Hispanics. According to the Census Bureau (2001c), "The federal government considers race and Hispanic origin to be two separate and distinct concepts." This means that people of Hispanic origin are represented in other categories, depending on how they identified their own race. A series of questions in the 2000 census did address the problem, and an estimated 12.5 percent of the population identified themselves as being of Hispanic origin. Percentages do not total 100 percent because of rounding.

In 2000, 50.9 percent of U.S. residents were female, and 49.1 percent were male (U.S. Census Bureau 2001b). The average age of the population was 35.3 years, with 25.7 percent of the population under 18, 39.8 percent between ages 25 and 44, 22.0 percent between ages 45 and 64, and 12.4 percent ages 65 and over (U.S. Census Bureau 2001a). Figure 9.2 shows the aging of America's population since 1900.

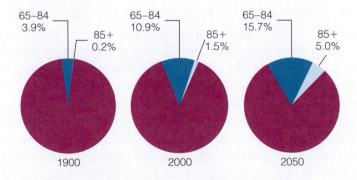

FIGURE **9.2**   **Aging of America, 1900, 2000, and 2050 (projected)** *Source: U.S. Census Bureau (2001a).*

Religious affiliations also demonstrate the diversity of the United States and the continuing viability of the First Amendment to the U. S. Constitution, which guarantees freedom of religion. Table 9.1 shows the results of a survey of religious identification taken in 2001.

TABLE 9.1   Religious Identification by Adults, United States, 2001

Response to "What is your religion, if any?"	Percent responding
Christian	
Catholic	24.5
Baptist	16.3
Methodist	6.8
Other Christian	28.9
Jewish	1.3
Buddhist	0.5
Islamic	0.5
Hindu	0.4
Unitarian	0.3
Other religion	0.7
No religion	14.1
Refused to answer	5.4

Source: Kosmin, Mayer, and Keysar (2001).

Notes: The data in this table are not taken from the census. As the Census Bureau (2005) explains on its site, Public Law 94-521 prohibits mandatory questions in the census on religious affiliation. Percentages do not total 100 percent because of rounding.

In many parts of the world, diversity has led to conflict between people of differing cultures and beliefs. The lessons of World War II and the Holocaust did not prevent the Troubles in Ireland, genocide in the former Yugoslavia and Rwanda, or ongoing violence in the Middle East. The United States was originally settled, in part, by Europeans escaping

religious intolerance. That did not stop them or the generations that followed from practic-ing religious intolerance themselves, from mistreating Native Americans, or from building a regional economy based on slavery. Unfortunately and despite legislation to the contrary, intolerance still exists in the United States in the form of hate crimes, prejudice, stereotyping, and discrimination against certain groups based on race, ethnic origin, religion, gender, age, disability, or sexual orientation. However, education and experience can help erase the hate.

During elementary or high school, you may have studied African-American culture during February, which is Black History month, or you may have studied women's history in March. St. Patrick's Day, Hanukah, Chinese New Year, and Cinco de Mayo are just a few other examples of the rich and diverse tapestry of culture celebrated in America and covered in school curricula. Use your college experience to broaden your perspective even further by learning more about people who are different from you.

Get Connected with Culture, Diversity, and Relationships

On a daily basis you have the opportunity in classes, labs, and campus activities to learn about and appreciate different cultures and the contributions of both men and women. This is your chance to begin building relationships with people from diverse cultures and backgrounds. If you are hesitant or don't know how to get started, try some of these strategies:

- Learn more about the history, customs, values, and beliefs of people who are different from you. The Internet, foreign language classes, world history or literature courses, Latino, African-American, or deaf studies classes, student club forums, or on-campus lectures and film series are good places to start.

- Set aside the stereotypes you may have about other races, cultures, or religions. Not all women are bad drivers, and not all men are addicted to ESPN. Value and interact with people as individuals, not as members of a group.

- Treat people who are different from you the way you would want to be treated. They may be as shy, nervous, or afraid of you as you are of them.

- Be tolerant of others. Their beliefs and feelings are just as important to them as yours are to you.

- Do not try to "fix" other people or to make them more like you. Advising, criticizing, and preaching are barriers that will prevent you from building relationships.

- Be patient. It takes time to get to know other people even if they are just like you. It also takes time to change and let go of any preconceived notions you or they may have.

- Enjoy the experience and treasure the education and knowledge you can get outside the classroom.

The more you know, the more you can appreciate the contributions that people of all races, cultures, backgrounds, and beliefs can make to your college experience, your profes-sional aspirations, and your personal life.

Get Connected with Technology: Integrity and Diversity Websites

The Internet can help you learn more about ethics and integrity, culture, relationships, and diversity. The following sites are just a few examples of what is available online:

- The Center for Public Integrity (http://www.publicintegrity.org), a nonprofit that focuses on inspiring a higher level of accountability from government and elected officials, is a source for investigative reports, current events, articles, and lobbying information.
- Read about famous people with disabilities, such as Tom Cruise, Magic Johnson, and Marlee Matlin, at http://www.familyvillage.wisc.edu/general/famous.html.
- The Office for Civil Rights of the U.S. Department of Education (http://www.ed.gov/about/offices/list/ocr/publications.html#ADDITI) has information about Title VI (race), Title IX (gender), and Section 504 (disability) discrimination.
- Information about religions and promoting religious tolerance can be found at http://www.religioustolerance.org.
- The U.S. Equal Opportunity Employment Commission (EEOC) (http://www.eeoc.gov) has information and laws on age and disability discrimination and sexual harassment.
- Take a self-assessment for hidden bias and read about ways to fight hate on campus at www.tolerance.org.

Get Connected with Reading: Drawing Logical Conclusions

As you research, read, and make notes on information, you draw logical conclusions about the topic. A *logical conclusion* is the judgment you make from the information presented. Your conclusions are based on the facts presented, stated and implied ideas, your knowledge and experience, and your interpretation of motives, reasons, and results. Authors, though, sometimes attempt to direct you to preconceived conclusions; therefore, it is important to keep the author's purpose and point of view in mind as you draw your conclusions.

The reasoning used to draw logical conclusions is called *inductive reasoning,* which consists of gathering facts, evidence, reasons, and proof—in the form of supporting details—and from that information developing a conclusion. The inductive-reasoning model (Figure 9.3) is in the shape of a triangle—narrow at the top and wider at the bottom—which reflects the process of moving from specifics (in the form of facts, evidence, reasons, and proof) to a general conclusion.

Drawing logical conclusions is a critical reading skill, necessary to analyze information, review trends, distinguish between similar circumstances, and predict future actions. You will find the inductive reasoning model used to draw logical conclusions very helpful in many of your course assignments. For example, if you were researching racial and ethnic profiling at border crossings or airports, you would first examine the facts, reasons, reports, and data from a number of varied sources. Then you would draw a conclusion based on all of the evidence as to whether or not the benefits of profiling outweigh the potential discriminatory impact.

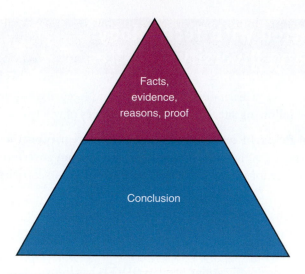

FIGURE **9.3**   **Inductive Reasoning Model**

Get Connected with Writing: Research Papers

There is no escape from writing research papers in college. Although you can turn out an essay in relatively quick order, a good research paper cannot be completed with just a few hours of work. You need a plan to do your best work and receive the grades you want to earn. As soon as you receive a research paper assignment, start thinking about your plan.

Divide the process into chunks, smaller segments that you can work on over a period of days or weeks. As you begin, you may be tempted to save time by skipping the preliminary steps. Don't. The time you spend limiting and defining your topic, framing your thesis statement, and drafting your outline is well spent and will save you time and effort later.

Choose a topic. To keep yourself motivated while you work on research papers, think about topics that interest you—subjects that you would like to learn more about. Then choose one of those from the broad subject categories that your professors usually assign.

Do preliminary research. Get an overview of the availability of source materials that address your topic. This overview will help you test the viability of your topic and help you narrow your focus. Google Scholar (http://scholar.google.com) is a good search engine to use; or you can search a database of journal articles (Academic Search Premier is one example), an online encyclopedia (the Encyclopedia Britannica Online or the Columbia Encyclopedia at www.bartleby.com), or an online library collection (like the Gale Virtual Reference Library) to determine whether or not your topic is appropriate. You do not need to take notes at this stage, but do jot down particularly good sources so you can revisit them when you begin your research in earnest.

Define your topic. You want to focus on a single problem, issue, or question: A topic that is too broad will likely overwhelm you and ultimately detract from the effectiveness of your paper.

Write your draft thesis statement. To help you develop your thesis statement and to focus your attention on the point of your research, you may find it helpful to frame your topic as a question. This question will not necessarily be the thesis statement in your final paper, but it should give you the ideas you need to get started researching.

Develop a working bibliography. A working bibliography is a collection of all of your research sources—books, magazines, journals, online articles, speeches, videotapes—any source of information used in your paper. Use your working bibliography to collect all of the information (titles, authors, publishers, volumes, pages, dates, URLs, site sponsors) that you will need for your citations, list of references, or "works cited" page.

Make your preliminary outline. This rough outline or list of items you want to include in your paper will help you focus your note taking. You do not want to waste your time and effort taking notes on material that is not relevant or that you will not use.

Take research notes. Use your outline items to focus your note taking. The sample note card (Figure 9.4) shows a format you can use when you take notes on index cards, paper, or on

FIGURE **9.4**   **Sample Research Note**

your computer. At the top of the card or page, note the outline item to which the information applies. Then include the source information and your notes. Figure 9.4 shows information for the introduction section of a research paper on racial and ethnic profiling at border crossings or airports. The source is a United States Supreme Court opinion, and the notes include a quotation that may be appropriate for that section of the outline.

While you are taking your research notes, remember to evaluate the trustworthiness and reliability of your sources. Look at the dates of publication, check the credibility of the source, and consider the author's purpose, point of view, and any bias the author may have.

Develop your final outline. Once your research is complete, review and revise your draft thesis statement. Next, review your preliminary outline and revise it by supplying more detail, gained as a result of your research. Organize your final outline in the order you want to present your ideas and research, because this is what you will use to guide you through the writing process, paragraph by paragraph.

Document your sources. To avoid plagiarism, you must acknowledge all of the research sources—books, journals, magazines, newspapers, websites, and recordings—that you rely on in your paper. There are two basic forms of documentation used in research papers: short text citations that are explained fully in a reference list, and endnotes referenced in the text by number. The style manual—APA, Chicago, CSE, MLA, Turabian—that your professor designates will dictate the form and format you use for in-text citations and reference lists (*The Chicago Manual of Style* 2003; *MLA Handbook for Writers of Research Papers* 2003; *Publication Manual of the American Psychological Association* 2001; *Scientific Style and Format* 1994; Turabian 1996).

Spending time developing a plan and following it will help you stay organized and focused when you work on major research projects and papers.

Get Connected with Online Help to Write Research Papers

The Internet and your computer are invaluable tools to make your research projects more convenient and manageable. To get help with writing research papers and citing sources, check your college's website and learning center or try one of these sites:

- Dakota State University (http://www.departments.dsu.edu/library/instruct.html) has online tutorials on research, evaluating information, electronic search techniques, citing sources, and resource guides for papers on particular subjects.

- Purdue University's guide to writing research papers (http://owl.english.purdue.edu/workshops/hypertext/ResearchW) includes drafting a thesis statement, developing an outline, writing a first draft, making revisions, and proofreading.

- Long Island University (http://liu.edu/cwis/cwp/library/workshp/citation.htm) offers color-coded guides that show where each piece of source information belongs in APA, MLA, AMA, Chicago, and Turabian citations.

These websites are only a few examples of what you can find on the Internet to help you research, write, and document papers.

Have You Connected? Self-Assessment

After completing Chapter 9, answer the following questions about what you have learned.

1. Explain these terms in your own words:

   Ethics: _____

   _____

   Integrity: _____

   _____

   Trust: _____

   _____

   Fairness: _____

   _____

2. What strategies can you use to connect with and build relationships with people from diverse cultures? _____

   _____

3. Which Internet sites have you searched for information about relationships, diversity, or writing research papers? _____

   _____

   _____

4. Describe the reasoning model that you can use to draw logical conclusions. _____

   _____

   _____

5. Explain your plan for writing research papers. _____

   _____

   _____

Chapter 9 Summary

Get Connected with Relationships

1. Ethics are the rules of conduct and morality that govern your behavior.
2. Integrity deals with your personal honesty and is among the standards of conduct expected of you by colleges. Being honest, fair, and trustworthy enables you to build beneficial relationships because you can be trusted.

3. College campuses bring together people of all ages, cultures, races, and beliefs providing the opportunity for students to build relationships and learn more about each other.

4. There are a number of strategies that you can use as you learn to make connections with people who are different from you.

5. The Internet is an invaluable aid for learning about integrity, diversity, and building relationships.

Get Connected with Reading: Drawing Logical Conclusions

1. Logical conclusions are opinions formed and judgments based on facts, evidence, reasons, and proof.

2. To draw logical conclusions, read the information carefully and analyze it in terms of the material in the reading and your own experience with the subject. Use an inductive reasoning model to guide you through the process.

Get Connected with Writing: Research Papers

1. Divide the tasks of working on a research paper into smaller, more manageable parts.

2. Before you begin your research, go through the following steps: select your topic, do preliminary research, define your topic, draft a thesis statement, develop a working bibliography, and create a preliminary outline. This process will help you research and take notes more efficiently.

3. To save time and effort later, use a working bibliography as you do your research, including all of the information about your sources that is required by the style manual you must use.

4. Revise your preliminary outline to create the final outline that you will use in writing your paper.

5. Internet sites can provide helpful guidance to organizing, drafting, and using citations in research papers.

References

"Affidavit: $90,000 Found in Congressman's Freezer." 2006. CNN.com http://www.cnn.com/2006/POLITICS/05/21/jefferson.search/index.html (accessed June 6, 2006).

Ahrens, Frank. 2005. "An Image Makeover: When Stewart Leaves Prison, She'll Try to Follow Others Who Have Salvaged Reputations." *Austin American Statesman,* March 2.

Barnes, David M. 2005. "Colleges Take Action to Stop File-Sharing." *Austin American Statesman,* September 23.

Bennett, Drake. 2004. "That Was Then . . . Steroids." *Boston Globe,* December 19.

Berkman, Johanna. 2001. "Steve Madden: Crisis of the Sole." New York. http://newyorkmetro.com/nymetro/news/bizfinance/biz/features/4406/index.html, February 26 (accessed December 18, 2005).

Bohls, Kirk. 2005. "Throw Raffy a Bone and a Wing in the Hall." *Austin American Statesman,* August 3.

Bridges, John. 2004. "The 2004 Hootie Awards: The Most Stupid Moments in Sports." *Austin American Statesman,* December 21.

Chandler, Susan. 2004. "Why Success Breeds Excess." *Chicago Tribune,* September 26.

The Chicago Manual of Style, 15th ed. 2003. Chicago: University of Chicago Press.

"Congressman Resigns after Bribery Plea." 2005. CNN.com. http://www.cnn.com/2005/POLITICS/11/28/cunningham, November 28 (accessed December 18, 2005).

Copelin, Laylan. 2005. "DeLay and His Legacy Are Both on Trial." *Austin American Statesman,* December 18.

DesJardins, Joseph R., and John J. McCall. 2005. *Contemporary Issues in Business Ethics.* 5th ed. Belmont, CA: Thomson Wadsworth.

Dominick, Joseph. 2002. *The Dynamics of Mass Communication: Media in the Digital Age,* 7th ed. New York: McGraw-Hill.

"Feeling Vindicated: He Beat It." 2005. *Austin American Statesman,* June 19.

Goleman, Daniel. 1995. *Emotional Intelligence.* New York: Bantam Books.

Geewax, Marilyn. 2005. "Court: Companies Liable for Illegal Downloading." *Austin American Statesman,* June 28.

Herring, Peg. 2006. "New Study Examines How Role Models Influence Ethical Behavior." Oregon State University News & Communication Service. http://oregonstate.edu/dept/ncs/newsarch/2006/jan06/ethics.htm (accessed June 6, 2006).

Jesdanun, Anick. 2005. "Battle over Copyrights Unfolding at Colleges." *Austin American Statesman,* May 30.

Kosmin, Barry A., Egon Mayer, and Ariela Keysar. 2001. "American Religious Identification Survey, 2001." New York: Graduate Center of the City University of New York. http://www.gc.cuny.edu/faculty/research_briefs/aris/key_findings.htm (accessed December 9, 2005).

Mankiw, N. Gregory. 2004. *Principles of Economics.* 3rd ed. Belmont, CA: Thomson Wadsworth.

MLA Handbook for Writers of Research Papers, 6th ed. 2003. New York: Modern Language Association.

"Newsmakers: Rapper Back in Court." 2005. *Austin American Statesman,* September 23.

Publication Manual of the American Psychological Association, 5th ed. 2001. Washington, DC: American Psychological Association.

Scientific Style and Format: The CSE Manual for Authors, Editors, and Publishers, 6th ed. 1994. New York: Cambridge University Press.

Seremet, Pat. 2004. "When Your Tried and True Pals Are Tried and Convicted." *Hartford Courant,* January 31.

Sheridan, Chris. 2004. "NBA Suspends Pacers' Artest for Season." *Austin American Statesman,* November 22.

"Smackdown Culture Runs Amok, Fed by Anger—and Money." 2004. *Austin American Statesman,* November 26.

Turabian, Kate L. 1996. *A Manual for Writers of Term Papers, Theses, and Dissertations,* 6th ed. Chicago: University of Chicago Press.

U.S. Census Bureau. 2001a. "Age and Sex: 2000." Census 2000 Summary File 1, Matrices PCT12 and P13. http://factfinder.census.gov/servlet/GCTTable?_bm=y&-geo_id=01000US&-_box_head_nbr=GCT-P5&-ds_name=DEC_2000_SFI_U&-lang=en&-format=US-9&-_sse=on (accessed December 9, 2005).

——.2001b. "Census 2000 Demographic Profile Highlights." Fact Sheet. http://factfinder.census.gov/servlet/SAFFacts?_sse=on (accessed December 9, 2005).

——. 2001c. "Overview of Race and Hispanic Origin 2000. Census Brief. C2KBR/01-1. http://www.census.gov/population/www/cen2000/briefs.html, March (accessed December 8, 2005).

——.2005. "Religion." http://www.census.gov/prod/www/religion.htm, February 15 (accessed July 10, 2005).

Photo Credits

Index